YOU HAVE ARRIVED

by Shannon Joy Mekeel

By Shannon Joy Mekeel

Produced by SJM Consulting Serviceshttps://sjmconsulting-services.co/

Edited by Lil Barcaski

Published by: GWN Publishing
www.GWNPublishing.com

Cover Design: End Zone Solutions

Print ISBN: 978-1-959608-69-1
Ebook ISBN: 978-1-959608-68-4

ADVANCED PRAISE FOR

YOU HAVE ARRIVED

When Shannon's life as a mom and professional—while supporting her husband with prostate cancer—became too stressful, she did what many of us wish we could do. She pressed the pause button and resigned from her corporate job. What came next was a 30-day adventure that changed her life forever. Shannon has this unique ability as a storyteller to weave personal and professional lessons into something very meaningful. She shares why listening to your small, quiet voice and journaling for clarity is so important for your sanity in today's busy world. She also has a knack for connecting people personally and professionally, and I know that as a consultant she is going to make huge waves.

Katy Rey, Entrepreneur + Author of Your Labels Don't Define You, YOU Define You. Organizer of CelebrateYOU

You Have Arrived combines relevant stories about the challenges our human family faces every day with the need for business to adopt a new way of viewing and working with these challenges. When you consider the personal trauma created by drug addictions, serious health challenges and the special struggles of a single parent family, leaders can no longer afford to turn a blind eye and pretend these issues do not exist. Shannon Mekeel's personal experiences in these areas, combined with multiple talents that improve profits and productivity, make her and *You Have Arrived* a combination that can transform the next generation of business into a more empathetic, and human-centric entity.

Sheyenne Kreamer, CE, Universal Soul-ution Alliance, Inc.

In *You Have Arrived*, Shannon masterfully combines her rich tapestry of experiences to offer invaluable lessons on finding balance and fulfillment at work and at home. Her approach to leadership—valuing employee growth, encouraging open dialogue, and her personal journey to find a healthy work-life balance—resonates deeply with the current needs of today's workforce. Shannon's unique ability to make decisions on the fly, her commitment to integrity, and her skill in fostering relatable connections shine through the pages. This book is a testament to her expertise, making it a must-read for anyone looking to grow their team or enhance employee engagement and development. Shannon's insights have not only inspired me but also reinforced the importance of leading with empathy and purpose.

Lindsey Freeman, Entrepreneur and founder of Two Hands Creative

In researching family histories, I often find situations where a person's path in life is drastically changed because of an event or series of events. I have uncovered situations where a death, a pregnancy, illness, or the loss of employment became a turning point in a person's life. Among the many situations faced by the author that are potentially life-altering, one of which is when her spouse is diagnosed with cancer, is especially difficult. The reality for anyone facing this crisis includes asking the question, "How will this affect me?" The response to a significant other's crisis is guided by the quality of the relationship, the depth of the burden, and the strength of our own mental health. The author's reaction reveals the journey she took in coping with her husband's illness and the raw feelings she experienced along the way.

Paul Kiser, Author and Genealogist

AUTHOR'S NOTE

Some will tell you that putting your secrets down for everyone to read is dangerous. Some will promise that if you are completely vulnerable and put it down on paper, others are bound to connect with your story, and if all goes well you will get the opportunity to help people. That should always be the goal: to help people.

This tale is about my becoming and my arrival. It is about being a mom, getting a divorce, climbing the corporate ladder, meeting the love of my life, and how friends can hold you up... and even mend your broken heart. The irony of my title, *You Have Arrived*, is that none of us ever really do arrive. Instead, we just do our best every day to be authentic and honor those who have gone before us. Sure, there are those big, beautiful moments when we sense the clouds parting and we reach the proverbial summit, but eventually, we must climb down the mountain, regroup, and walk toward our next goal to arrive once more. Those who live life to the fullest achieve greatness by helping others, and in so doing we can arrive each day, and that's what makes life such a gift; not arriving per se but getting the opportunity to serve and to evolve.

Women of every culture must face extreme challenges unlike those of our male counterparts. This is just the stuff of life. Women have this amazing way of leaning on their girlfriends—I like to refer to mine as my mermaids—and for that reason alone we are starkly different than men in dealing with problems.

Women have been uniquely equipped to create hope, home, and new human life, and when life gets really hard, we pray, we sing, we dance, and eventually we reach out to our confidants for advice and support. To "take shit in stride," was something I was told to do at the age of sixteen by the first boy I fell for. Ever since then, I have been categorically taking my shit in stride. I am confidently equipped at this point to handle whatever life throws at me, with a little help from my friends, that is.

When faced with adversity, often, what results from my navigating tumultuous times is better than anyone could have expected. You could also look at it like this: her life was in the toilet. She flushed it, despite everyone's doubt that she had long enough reach or even the strength in her body to do so, and as soon as she decided to pull the handle, miraculously, just as she suspected, good things started to happen. A pleasant swoosh sound filled the room. The water flowed evenly and strongly from small holes hidden around the rim of the bowl. That flush was working in perfect synchrony for her. *Wow. Thanks, Universe!* The water spiraled in a clockwise direction, and just when things seemed dizzying, a switch pulled... and the chaos was over. The water started to refill, and things looked clearer and cleaner than ever before. The filth that had been a part of her life for way too long was now gone and what was left was a clean slate. The flush just worked perfectly.

TABLE OF CONTENTS

Advanced Praise for *3*

Author's Note *5*

Preface *9*

1: Family First *15*

2: The Guy from Idaho *25*

3: Ancient History *28*

4: Our Happy Home *47*

5: The Gift of The Nervous Breakdown *58*

6: Embraced at Mount of Olives *62*

7: Equilibrium *77*

8: My Roman Warrior... Sigh *93*

9: Conan *108*

10: PC to Gainesville & Back Again *122*

11: Becoming *154*

12: The Small, Quiet Voice *167*

13: It Is Time to Rethink the American Dream *185*

14: Momming *196*

15: Tom Bodell Said He'd Leave the Light on For You (But We'll Kick You Out at Eleven) *205*

16: Finding Joy *210*

17: The Storyteller ... 214
18: Final Pink Feminist Thoughts ... 217
Dedications ... 222
About the Author ... 229

PREFACE

Remember those books that we all read when we were kids called *Curious George*, written by Margret and Hans Rey and illustrated by Alan Shalleck?[1] They were my favorites when I was a little girl, and I read them to my siblings, as well as my own three sons. *Curious George* was also a favorite at the preschools that I taught at when I was a young mother. The title "preschool teacher" is one of the many occupations I have held that is not on my resume, but I learned so much from those two years; like empathy in its purest form, epitomized during the time the little ones looked forward to most of all, circle time. To see the children's eyes light up when their hero was victorious, and their foreheads furrow with concern when trouble was afoot, these were the purest of emotions. Little ones can't help but love and relate to that silly little monkey that the authors first called "Fifi" in their original manuscript.

Recently, much has been written about the authors of the seven *Curious George* books that have sold more than twenty-five million copies over the last four generations. Margret and Hans Rey were childhood sweethearts from Hamburg Germany. They were both from Jewish families and living in Paris when they worked on their first book. The couple was about to publish their manuscript when the Nazis invaded Paris in 1940. The couple fled

1 *Galchen, Rivka. The Unexpected Profundity of Curious George. The New Yorker, 3 June 2019, www.newyorker.com/books/page-turner/ the-unexpected-profundity-of-curious-george.*

France and made their way through Europe to eventually end up in New York with no more than the clothes on their back, and their manuscript. It was the only thing that mattered.

Pick up any *Curious George* book and you can see that the drawings are simple, and the stories are outwardly charming, but the Reys risked their very lives smuggling their work out of Europe. They both knew what they had created was more than the average book for kids. They had created something special that the world needed right then. Fifi's lessons would be their legacy, and although it was just a children's book, the Reys fully believed their work could help children around the world feel less afraid.

They were successful in bringing *Curious George* to market over the next two and a half decades. All seven books have been embraced and celebrated by parents and children because they provide a simpler view of the world. But superficial cuteness would not be enough to set these stories apart for four generations if they were not indeed extraordinary.

Margret and Hans wrote about what they knew, as they had lived extraordinary lives in Paris and Rio De Janeiro. They were eccentric... so much so that they even took their pair of pet marmoset monkeys with them on their honeymoon. Because the books they wrote were for young minds with limited attention spans, the authors' focus was always on whimsical and short problems with quick resolutions. For their readers, who are often impetuous, the authors knew that these types of plots would build optimism and confidence. They were teaching kids that, just like George, despite the challenges they may face in their own lives, they too would be okay.

For over eighty years *Curious George* books have been a useful tool for good child indoctrination. But take a closer look, and encompassed in all that monkeying around are some very serious moral lessons. All of this is folded up into a neat little package that kids love; the appealing phrases, short bursts of endorphins, and pleasant primary-colored illustrations. The most important part is this; always as George's rescuer, The Man with the Yellow Hat, saves the day... EVERY SINGLE TIME.

The Man's consistency to show up for his monkey is admirable, especially when one considers that George is perpetually defiant, and usually takes advantage of his caretaker. In my opinion, the dynamic between George and The Man with the Yellow Hat is the most profound way the authors influence young readers. It is yet another brilliant layer of the psychological theme the Reys utilized. In case you were wondering where I am going with this, the Reys were both advertising executives and built their careers on their ability to understand and profit from the science of marketing. That discipline, as I see it, is to tap into societal trends consistently and sufficiently predict and produce profit, and the Reys knew how to do just that. They were qualified to bring *Curious George* to life, not because they had children of their own, but because they made it their life's work to know what parents and kids needed, at that point in time and more importantly, what consumers would buy.

There is a lot of psychology that goes into marketing, and I think that is what makes it so much fun. You could argue that marketers are manipulators, but I think most of us just hope to spin and sell products in a way that serves humanity. The pitfall that people don't often talk about, however, is that marketers can lose their creative juice when they focus too much of their energy on ROI (return on investment). When that happens, they lose sight of the beauty of it all. I won't for a moment profess that my struggles could be compared with those of the Reys. After all, I didn't have Nazis to contend with... but the struggle to bring my first book out of the ether has been monumentally difficult, as you will soon discover.

The point that I want to drive home to you by introducing you to the Reys is this; when Margaret and Hans refocused just enough of their collective energy away from their high-stress advertising jobs, they were able to create, arguably, one of the best children's book series of all time, and their side hustle ended up being the project they would be remembered for. *Curious George* mattered more than any other campaign they ever worked on during their day job. So, in the spirit of being a journalist and not just a marketer, I want to be as transparent with you as possible. These are my memoirs, and I am pulling them from my memory and the recollection of those closest to me. This is why I have remembered everything over the years... because since I was fifteen, I knew that I was a journalist. I knew someday I would have time to write it all down, so I had to remember.

This project has been a deep dive into my psyche, so I get to make the rules and I sincerely believe that you will get a lot of value from what I have shared, especially in those in-between sections where I use authorial intrusion. During those moments, I will be speaking directly to you. I believe that this type of dialogue will also make this feel less like a book, and more like a conversation with someone fascinating that you just sat down next to during a two-hour flight.

So, now that I am well into my fourth month of writing, I have been trying to figure out how to best package these one-on-one conversations you and I will be having. It is important that you understand our conversations are of paramount importance. In a way, YOU will be helping me write this book. So, here it is, when things get stressful or scary, I'll insert italicized text, to give you a strong indicator that I'm here for you—just like the Man in the Yellow Hat was there for George—to assure you that there is a lesson to be learned from all these shenanigans.

Welcome to *You Have Arrived!*

"Another world is not only possible; she is on her way. On a quiet day I can hear her breathing."

— Arundhati Roy

"Sometimes my walk looks strange, but it's that way for a Reason...and I still have to walk it."

— Me, 4-20-2023

"What if Joy is the only metric of my success? If you are not used to seeing joy and the effects that it has on people's lives, when it finally comes along, it can be strange and scary."

— Me, 4-28-2023

If Not Now, When?

Embrace Your Nervous Breakdown

YOU Are More Than Enough... I Promise.

FOR ALL THE MERMAIDS

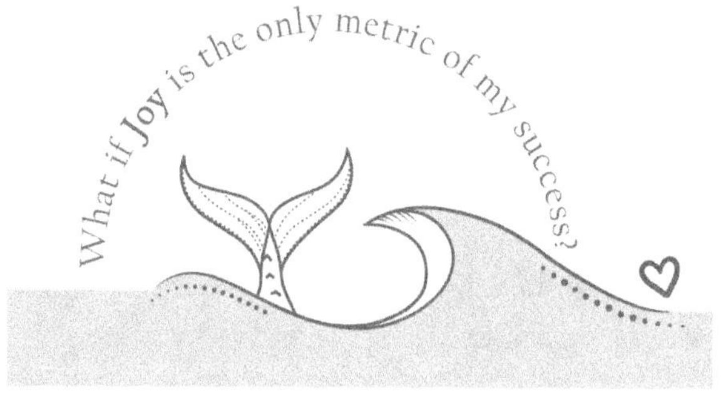

Names and places have been changed, when necessary, but AI was not used in any portion of this book because robots don't have childhood trauma. This book is a memoir, but it is also an organizational resource designed to inspire further learning. I encourage you to utilize the links to the articles provided, as they substantiate issues employees face and offer practical ways to support improvements in workplace culture.

CHAPTER 1

FAMILY FIRST

Isn't it strange how naive we can be when we don't listen? Isn't it embarrassing when we refuse to see and hear the whole story? Knowing only half-truths about my family's history has plagued me most of my adult life. I joined the Air Force right after high school and didn't get the opportunity to ask questions or learn the adult versions of the stories that defined me as a person until very recently. I thought I had originally written the last word of my book when I was driving home from visiting friends in Fort Lauderdale. I called my dad on the afternoon of April 28th and proclaimed my book to be done and this insane time in my life to be over.

He had no idea what we had been going through since my husband Tony's prostate cancer treatment had started six weeks prior. Neither my dad nor I could have guessed that my crazy ride was, in fact, just getting started... but I digress.

The sun was setting on this marshy, odd terrain and I felt like the sun was also setting on this very hard time in my life. I could finally go home now and hug my husband because I had come up with a plan and I had gained clarity about it all. With tears in my eyes... and as a diversion to completely breaking down, I asked my dad about what he remembered when he was young. I also wanted to know about one of the most elusive stories in our family, the fascinating tale of his birth. When my request left my lips, I had a feeling there was more to the story. As a girl, I had been told that my dad was born two months early, and he was so tiny that my grandmother had used men's handkerchiefs folded in quarters to diaper him. I tried to imagine how he was able to survive as a four-pound, eight-week, premature infant in 1949, and I could not fathom it.

After all, over the years, I have known a lot of moms to give birth to tiny preemies. Even now, some don't survive despite extreme medical interventions, and as a mother to three grown sons, I was finally asking important questions. I had a reason. I was on a quest to learn more about my lineage and the first story I wanted to hear was how my dad had survived those odds in 1949. I spent my career in marketing and as a journalist and yet I had failed to ask some of the most significant questions about my own family. What did that make me? Distracted? Definitely. A hypocrite? Maybe.

I was a woman who loved her family very much, but I didn't have any idea of where I really came from. My origin story was ghost whispers, and my lineage had become a thin slice of Swiss cheese, incomplete and insignificant. But it shouldn't be like this. All my grandma ever did was TELL STORIES. The thought of not knowing these stories any longer became unacceptable. So, as any good journalist does, I started asking questions of anyone who knew anything about my family's history, and then I booked a flight to Colorado to get the scoop.

Here is what I discovered in my research: My grandma gave birth to three sons, at home, rather easily, and she expected a repeat performance with her fourth son, my father. But that would not be the case. She went into labor eight weeks too soon with my dad and his birth would be traumatic. In fact, she nearly died bringing him into the world.

I needed to find out more about my family, and truthfully, life had been so busy over the past thirty years that I had forgotten to ask the questions. It's what happens when kids move away. As brave, young adults, we cash in our ticket to adventure and opportunity, but we also sacrifice ever getting to know the adult version of the stories that defined our family... that define us and how we fit into the world.

Leaving home when I was eighteen and joining the Air Force was a decision I made based on fear and desperation. I so wanted to prove everyone wrong and make something of myself. I visit my family in Colorado when I can, but I am largely an outsider when it comes to family dynamics, holidays, and conversations... and that makes me sad sometimes. Knowing the stories that shaped my family and those who lived generations before me was something I wanted, but until *You Have Arrived*, I didn't have a reason or permission to ask the questions.

I am happy that I took the time to breathe and to learn more about my family and myself because we all deserve that time and few of us take it. The truth is, I had my nervous breakdown and I learned from it. Now I can share what I have learned.

Eight months into this project and the weather has changed from spring; a frantic breaking open of my heart, into summer; a season of discovery and deep searching, and finally the rain is once again changing the landscape. I sit in my local Starbucks as I type this, and a light drizzle falls on the window outside. The season of light is upon us and the red Christmas cup I was gifted by my barista is proof positive of that fact. Eight is my lucky number and it's been eight months. The book could not have been finished in a month and it could not have been completed in six months... but now? Now I have received sage advice from the loving patriarch of my family, and I realize that it is time to pivot.

The process of writing it all down has been cathartic, and through processing my full truth with a few family members and friends, I have realized what this project must become, and what I want to do with the rest of my life. What a gift the rain has been to me. My original manuscript read as a journal, and as one does in their journal, I complained a lot about things that I have been through personally and professionally. It did not, however, offer much advice on how to rise above it.

Who am I, after all, to offer advice? I am a veteran, and an experienced mid-level manager who is good at her job and fiercely passionate about human rights, but I lack the credentials of "doctor," and that is what our society needs, a doctor to fix the mess we have gotten ourselves into. But as I gathered my mermaids, someone fluttered back into my life and became my mentor, life coach, and business partner. And you are not going to believe this, but she is EXACTLY who I needed to enable this book to be a resource to you, and not just a childish rant.

I met LauraLynn Jansen in 2012 while I was working as a lifestyle magazine editor. She was running a paddle board yoga shop and aerial yoga studio on Panama City Beach. During our interview, I was instantly attracted to her energy. She is one of the most empathetic, kind, understanding, and wise people I have ever met. LauraLynn is just easy to be around. People flock to her. After her feature article came out, I was blessed that she and I became friends. Then when she and I both moved from the Florida Panhandle we kept in touch over the years on social media, Christmas cards, and inspirational text messages and calls whenever we were drawn to reach out to one another.

How appropriate that I introduce her to you in this chapter, "Family First," since she is a member of my chosen family. Those are the people we need in our lives to guide us and love us for who we really are. Her friendship has been no less than life-changing for me. She sees and recognizes me, and she acknowledges me, and that has made all the difference, especially this year when everything has changed.

Since our time together on the Emerald Coast LauraLynn has been living in some of the most beautiful places, including Hawaii, Colorado, and Germany, she has also been supporting her wife who is an officer in the USAF. She and Shannon were together under "Don't Ask, Don't Tell," and have always been supporters of transparency and truth in military relationships. After all, whether Shannon loves a man or a woman, it does not matter. Shannon is fully supported by her spouse and that is the most important thing regarding a healthy active-duty relationship steeped in stress and constant personification of service before self.

So now that you know "who" Laura Lynn is, let me tell you what she has been up to, besides coaching me. She just completed her dissertation to the faculty of the Graduate School of Leadership and Change at Antioch University and has now earned her Ph.D. She is now a Doctor of Philosophy and her brilliant dissertation, is called "Moksa, Seeking a Humanizing Way of Being: I am Recognized. I am Acknowledged. I am Human."[2]

The important work that she has been doing perfectly aligns with the reasons that I paused my life to write this book in the first place, so I intend to honor Dr Jansen's work by including excerpts from her dissertation. As I offer my own stories of personal vulnerability, these stories will be met with professional advice from someone I trust completely and someone who I know will change the world. Here is Dr. Jansen's intro to her

2 *Jansen, L. (2023). Mok a, Seeking a Humanizing Way of Being: I am Recognized. I am Acknowledged. I am Human. https://aura.antioch.edu/etds/978*

dissertation. I hope you are as excited as I am to learn from her. This is going to be fun!

"This dissertation delves into the intricate dimensions of humanization by shifting the analytical focus from denial and exclusion to affirmative aspects of inclusion. The central aim of this research is to unravel the mechanisms underlying the process of humanization, or how individuals perceive and internalize their being recognized as human beings." You have arrived at a place where chaos is met by calm, Namaste.

I discovered that I wanted to be a journalist—a truth teller—during my sophomore year of high school. I also knew early on that I would write a book, although I didn't know what that book would be about for a long time. I have remembered things that other people don't generally keep in their mind's cabinet, so the research for this project has been going on for the past thirty years.

As I grew up, joined the military, became a wife and mother, and worked for over a dozen employers over the years, I have been trying to navigate the world, like we all must, to survive. I have been gainfully employed since I was fifteen and life is what happens outside of those pursuits. Thinking, ruminating, and processing deep, old feelings has never been possible until now, because this is the first time in my life that I have permitted myself to pause.

I resigned from my stressful corporate job in May of 2023 and since then I have been working for and on myself. It is my sincere hope that by honoring this time, defining my values, and finishing this project, I can give you a peek into how I got to this stage in my life because I believe a lot of us need to make some major adjustments to our courses. In the next stage of my career, I consider myself blessedly enlightened. This is what I want to share with you because I am very excited about what I have learned.

My undergraduate degree was in marketing, and I have always wanted to pursue a master's degree program, but I couldn't decide what I wanted to pursue, although I knew it would be something in the study and service of people. After I started writing this book and developing the business plan for my consultancy firm, which is what I am passionate about, the "what" regarding the next stage of my career suddenly became very clear. At a lot of jobs I held, and at the job I had over the last six years, I had been the implementation guru. In carrying out those duties I realized that it is the systems and operations that directly impact the people within an organization, and that is what really matters to me... developing and optimizing good work.

So, through the study of processes, workplace culture can become less about ambiguous and unattainable perks and fluff than it is about the policies, procedures, and roadblocks that employees deal with every day. Moreover, the principle of, "do the right thing" doesn't change depending on which generation you talk to. Baby Boomers and those born in 1965-1979 like me, categorized as Gen X have always expected their employers to do the right thing and indeed, many improvements have been made over the past two generations, of which I will provide examples in this and subsequent chapters. In each generation, because ideas are shared, we get a little better in some ways. We learn things, sure, but sometimes apathy creeps in creating new varieties of toxicity. I believe that is where we are now.

My sons' generations, Millennial and Gen-Z have had the advantage of parents who are transparent with them. That's our way. We treat our kids like friends because we want to teach them to be better than us and we know that sharing transparency and empathy are how to do that. Those under thirty, in many cases, have also witnessed the hours, the stress, and the lack of compensation that has plagued their parents and their grandparents' generations and they are not signing up for that.

Another key difference between us and them is that those under the age of thirty are the first generation that is intimately connected through constant streams of thought from their peers through social media. Americans under thirty don't consume news and entertainment from the popular press. Many young people don't trust the major networks or newspapers because they know these news outlets have been corrupted and manipulated. No, this new generation of Americans, which now comprises over half of our population, is organized, intelligent, informed, and they are just.

They are on the same page with their peers and if they remain that way, this generation has the capability of changing the course of our nation in a multitude of positive ways. The traditional patriarchy is already being rejected as minorities and women now have seats at all the tables. My middle son, Ryan who is 22 urges, "Stop thinking in terms of Democrats and Republicans, conservatives or liberals, and start looking at it (the division of our society) as working class versus the ruling class." Our culture is shifting, and I am excited about what's to come.

But as a mother of three sons under twenty-six who question everything, know everything, and truthfully want very little from others, how could I impact what I knew the most about; the modern workplace, in a way that would help young people and the current regime improve their communication, processes, and philosophies in a way that moves us closer to our goals as a nation?

The answer to that question is what you hold in your hands. I intend to share some very personal life stuff about me and my family and friends because as employers and colleagues, it's vital to remember that everyone you meet, manage, or employ is the center of their own universe and they are all going through something monumental, pivotal, challenging, and life-changing right now.

How can those of us who consider ourselves productive and competitive professionals take time out of our busy day to deal with it all, and when necessary, help our subordinates navigate their lives' issues? It's not going to be easy, but we absolutely must find a way to renegotiate our time and do just that, however.

Here is the bottom line: empathy is what is lacking in our workplaces in the U.S. We lack basic empathy, not because we don't care about others, but because we are all too busy, mentally strained, and self-absorbed. It's why in Dr. Jansen's dissertation she mentions empathy fifty-three times to describe the process of humanization, which she says, "has a chance to thrive when an interaction is set up for healthy risk-taking and supported by mutual empathy."[3]

So where do we go from here on the way to our arrival? Let's take a peek at the front cover. On the very top it says, "A Roadmap to Empathy, as Stories Light the Way." Buckle up, friend. Let's get real and be vulnerable! It's going to be a bumpy ride!

Through all my hustling, although I might have been having fun, I wasn't processing my truth, and I am going to tell you all about it. I had been compartmentalizing my stress, my fears, and my past trauma and no one could pull me out of that system except my small, quiet voice (whom you will get to know very well

3 *Jansen, L. (2023, p. 55). Moksa, Seeking a Humanizing Way of Being: I am Recognized. I am Acknowledged. I am Human. https://aura.antioch.edu/etds/978*

soon enough). I had to press the pause button to move forward in any aspect of my life. I could not physically resist that pause one moment longer, and I know that the reason I got to that point, is that the hustle culture has become our cultural norm.

Most American workers feel like I do and it's only a matter of time before we each pop in one way or another. I quit my job, and others may pick up a gun. Still, others successfully repress their angst, but it manifests as disease. Why is it like this in America? It isn't like this in other countries, but this is our normal and we have to start changing if we are going to move forward as a society. I believe that with every cell in my body.

So, we are going on this adventure together and you will get a wide windshield view of my life. In many ways I am the typical American woman, but I am also someone who cares deeply about effecting change and someone who has made a career out of examining and improving workplace systems.

My life makes a good case study because I started my career in the military and since then I have measured each organization that I worked for by the Air Force's core values of "Integrity First," "Service Before Self," and "Excellence in All We Do." Most organizations in the profit sector fail miserably at measuring up to these standards, and after 23 years I have figured out why.

In March of 2023, I experienced a convergence of over a dozen of the typical life stressors that psychologists say can cause a woman to have a nervous breakdown. I will be vulnerable about this time in my life because I want to increase your empathy toward your subordinates and colleagues. Perhaps my story can be the light that you need to turn your organization around.

CHAPTER 2

THE GUY FROM IDAHO

When we met at the Metro nightclub in Modesto California in the winter of 1992, we already knew our base was in the process of closing. Castle AFB was a casualty of the Base Realignment and Closure Commission following the end of the Cold War and the disestablishment of Strategic Air Command. To say morale was low at Castle in the early nineties was an understatement.

This was my first base and Elijah's second assignment. The parties held in the barracks were as frequent as they were wild, and soon, the security police would put the squeeze on underage drinking. A few of our friends were busted at a party just down the hall from my dorm and they were sentenced to ninety days in correctional custody. Elijah and I narrowly dodged a bullet that night. If we hadn't left when we did, we would have joined our friends marching in formation and picking up trash around the base.

Soon after that, we stopped staying where it was convenient, and we moved off base. I was only eighteen and didn't fully understand what it meant to be a responsible adult, but when I first visited Elijah's bachelor pad after dating him for several weeks, I had my suspicions that my new handsome and fun boyfriend might be failing in the 'adulting department.' Elijah had been opting to stay with me in my dorm in a single bed for a while because he loved me, and it was easier for him to get to work if he stayed on base. He would just start walking in the direction of the bomb dump and a buddy would pick him up on their way to work every day.

Then one Sunday, after we had spent nearly two months together, I visited Elijah's house off-base. He shared the duplex with two other guys from the bomb dump and they were hosting a Super Bowl party. When I first got to the house and looked around a bit, I began to have doubts about the maturity level of my much older boyfriend. How long had he lived here? There were still unpacked boxes in his room. I continued to nose around the bachelor pad without anyone noticing, and throughout the day I counted three books of checks with his name on them, none of which were in the vinyl covers with the bank register section that was used to record the checks you write. Was he even keeping track?

Then I saw a photo on the kitchen table of Elijah standing in front of a cute little white sports car parked in his parents' driveway. When I asked him about the car, he told me it had recently been repossessed. He hadn't made his payments, and as banks do, they took it back. I realize that these important discoveries should have been huge red flags for me. I should have run the other way, but all his transgressions were explained away with logical and reassuring excuses that I accepted as facts.

Elijah met most of my requirements for a life partner. I had written them down, and all but one he fulfilled: "He must be honest." But no matter. I was sure that I could change him. After all, no one is perfect. He loved me and I was glad to not be out in the world all alone. I was a young woman, essentially alone, living in California. I needed someone. At least that's what I thought. He was twenty-five and I was nineteen when we were married on July 4, 1994, on my mom and stepdad's front lawn in Craig,

Colorado. The decision to get married so young, and not just live together, was our only option if we were to be stationed as a couple. Because Castle was closing, everyone we knew was being reassigned somewhere in the next two years, and the only way to guarantee he and I would stay together was to get married. We had a dog. We were in love. So, that is what we did.

In the winter of 1994, when I picked up our orders from the base personnel office, my first call was not to my new husband, but rather to my mom. I found an open door to an office down the hall and darted in to call her. It was the middle of the day, and she picked up after two rings. She always picked up. "Mom, you are not going to believe this, but we got Fairchild!" "What? That's awesome. You are going to LOVE it there," she said. Out of all the places the Air Force could have sent the two of us, I could not believe we would soon be reassigned to Spokane, Washington. My urgency to call my mom and not my new husband when I learned the news, was because Fairchild had been the same base my parents had met and worked at before they had me. For the next six years, Elijah and I would work in the same buildings that my parents had worked in, twenty years prior. The coincidence was surreal.

Looking back, I realize that my time in the USAF gave me validation that I was part of something greater than myself. What I learned during those very hard six weeks of basic training was profound and in effect, it was the most humanizing experience I had experienced in my young life. I finally belonged and my eight years in the military would be defined by deep intrapersonal bonds. Going to my first duty station, and meeting Elijah and my other friends was the happiest time in my life. I felt as if I had arrived. Then, moving to Spokane and continuing my career and life as a young, married, enlisted woman was a launch into adulthood that was admirable, as well as exhilarating.

CHAPTER 3

ANCIENT HISTORY

Despite my grandma, my dad, and my aunt and uncles' constant storytelling at family gatherings, I had never really heard any stories about my parents when they were starting out in Washington State. I knew I was born into a loving relationship in Bellingham, Washington, but that was about all I really knew. The oldest daughter of two divorced hippies, the details of my first few years had always been just outside of my reach, gauzed in a type of mystery that I wasn't permitted to speak of.

My parents had remarried when I was nine, and I didn't want to upset either side of my new family. There was so much to be happy about, and as children, my sister and I played and went to school, and we were too young to remember anything bad. This was just our normal. So, I didn't ask. As we got older, life as the oldest of five kids with two sets of parents was complicated and electrically charged at every turn. I didn't have the bandwidth for the past then, and when I joined the Air Force for greener pastures and left town, I gave up being in the tribe. I was so detached and that's how it's always been for me.

It seemed that knowing what had happened in my mom and dad's lives wasn't important to anyone but me. But wasn't my need to know a good enough reason, now? I needed validation of my existence. Truly, it wasn't until I started writing You Have

Arrived that I had the time to honor the small voice inside that had been telling me to find out what happened during those years.

After Elijah and I had been in Spokane a full decade, raising the boys, my mom came out for a visit to welcome baby Ethan into the world. I was only four days postpartum, and mom thought it would be a good idea for me to drive our station wagon thirty minutes outside of town with two little boys, a newborn, and her riding shotgun. Mom was bored and just wanted to get out of the house, so we headed out to our favorite place to take the boys, a family farm co-op called Green Bluff, just north of Spokane.

Despite my apprehension about it being too much, we had a lovely day under the sun and cherry trees, with Ethan in my sling, and the boys playing with their grandma whom they rarely got the chance to see, much less make beautiful memories with. I have treasured photos of Mom and Ryan, who was three at the time, taken from behind, the pair of them in overalls, walking hand in hand through the orchard. When we had picked as many cherries as we thought we would be able to eat over the next week, we drove to a little church on a hill and spread a blanket out under a big shade tree. After we unwrapped the boys' sandwiches and got their juice packs poked, Mom said, quite matter-of-factly and completely out of the blue, "I want to tell you about when you were a baby, and I was a new Mom."

What? Here and now and without any prodding? This is where, and this is the time she has chosen to tell me all these things I have been waiting to hear about my entire life. But, oh gosh… I am holding a baby, and I don't have a pen!

Fact-checking can be a dangerous business, especially when people don't want to revisit times in their lives that are painful. When I called my mom in the fall of 2023 to ask her if I had remembered and written down correctly all the details of what she told me at our picnic nearly twenty years ago, she said, emphatically,

"Well, no." So, I started to ask her questions to correct the details. I had all these notions of my mom in my head for twenty years based on that day at Green Bluff. I had painted a picture of a young, free-spirited hippie with a young daughter in tow, trying to do the best she could do, despite a challenging cultural wave. We had bonded that day. Maybe I had heard her wrong then or maybe Mom's story had changed over the years. But whatever happened regarding this discrepancy, for nearly twenty years, I had been carrying around that picture Mom had painted for me that day after picking cherries. They had been facts then, but now that they had been recused, I felt shaken. Even robbed. What really happened?

Understand that all of this is ancient history and these years were filled with wild living and heartache. Because of this, no one has ever talked about these times that proved my family unit ever existed. The truth of the matter was that my family was broken when I was four and everyone was okay with this reality except for me and maybe my sister. The remnants of our family were put back together with two more actors five years later, so I never asked about what happened and no one volunteered this information, but I still needed to know. I should have heard these stories as I was growing up because not having any history of my mom and dad's existence together made me feel worse than just a kid with divorced parents. Not knowing where I came from invalidated me as a complete person. Because of this, as I was growing up, I didn't feel good enough or as if I belonged in most rooms unless I was visiting my grandma, of course. There, we all felt like we belonged.

LESSON: *Tell the love story to your kids, even if it ended abruptly.*

It's worth noting that the feeling of belonging is central to mental health and the development of one's true sense of humanization.

Being socially discounted or dismissed tends to leave individuals feeling less than human. According to Dr Jansen's research regarding the conceptual roots of critical consciousness, she looks to Brazilian educator and theorist Paulo Freire. He asserted that "the thinking subject exists about others in the world and that critical consciousness involves a reflective analysis of the differences in power present in social relationships and institutions." Dr Jansen professes, "Systemic situations can manipulate individual experiences of belonging and exclusion within intrapersonal and interpersonal levels. Developing the ability to resist and reject these manipulations and the resulting definition placed upon the stigmatized individual, are part of cultivating a critical consciousness.[4]

In the summer of 1970, *Mama Told Me (Not to Come)* by Three Dog Night was the most popular song on the radio. The Apollo 13 mission launched to the moon, and on the last day of the year, The Beatles disbanded. Hundreds of thousands protested the Vietnam War in Washington DC, and the voting age was lowered to eighteen. President Nixon was visited by Elvis at the White House, and he also signed the Occupational Safety and Health Act into Law, which would transform the American workplace. The world was a tinderbox of change that could ignite at any moment. It was difficult to be young and alone in the world, and so far away from family. That was the summer that my mom and dad were married in a simple ceremony at a judge's house on the South Hill of Spokane, Washington. She wore a pleated pink dress, and he a navy-blue double-breasted suit.

"You know how your dad is right? "Well," she said, "He was even more of a child then. He just wanted to party, but I had a baby. I

4 *LauraLynn, Jansen,. "Moksa, Seeking a Humanizing Way of Being: I Am Recognized. I Am Acknowledged. I Am Human." AURA - Antioch University Repository and Archive, 2023, aura.antioch.edu/ etds/978. Accessed 12 Dec. 2023.*

had you, and I wanted to be a good mom. I was unhappy, many times there wasn't enough money, and then I met someone else." She took her first bite of her turkey sandwich. I stayed silent and waited for her to chew. Then Mom popped a huge, warm cherry into her mouth, moaned about how yummy it was, and spit out the pit. Then she continued to tell me the story of when I was born and a few more juicy details about the first few years of my life.

That day at our picnic, the story was different from the facts she confirmed in the fall of 2023. So much has happened since then, but these were the only two occasions in my life when I heard any sort of explanation from her about what happened from 1970 -1975. Now my mom was seventy-three years old and dealing with some pretty serious health concerns. She certainly wasn't the same woman she was when she and my dad were starting out, and she wasn't even the same woman she had been under that big shade tree in 2004.

When I would speak with her on the phone each week from Florida, I would give her the highlights of our lives and she would tell me about her frequent doctor's appointments. Mom knew I was writing a book about my life, and she was oddly aloof about it. I thought she would be elated that her journalist daughter was taking on her greatest creative process by writing her memoir. Mom is an avid reader, despite near blindness, so I thought she would be happy that in some way, You Have Arrived would immortalize her.

So, upon learning that I had gotten the details wrong, I asked her to help me fill in the blanks about my first year for the book, and the tone of her voice changed. She couldn't understand why I would care so much about her life. She rationalized and told me as such. "If you can't remember things that happened when you were a baby, you shouldn't care. There was no abuse or anything,

Shannon." But as the oldest child in our family, I knew exactly where each of my siblings had been born and what happened when they were babies. I was there and I could be that storyteller for them.

Or maybe my need to know stemmed from my own mothering instincts. When my boys were little, before they could tell me if something was wrong, I was reluctant to let anyone outside our family babysit them. Little ones are fragile, and they can't tell you if they are being mistreated.

Mom just wanted me to trust that she had taken care of me when I was a baby... before I could remember the details of my life. And for a long time, that was enough for me. I did trust her to care for me because she was and is an excellent mother to all of us. But I still wanted to know... and I felt like it was selfish for her to keep this information from me. It wasn't just her history. It was OUR history—my mom's, my dad's, and mine—and I yearned to know not just the circumstances of my first three years, and the circumstances leading up to my birth but the journalist inside me needed to know the WHY too.

She pushed back, "Why do you care so much about my life? It's ancient history." Mom clearly loathed my curiosity about this time in her life, but she at last relented. According to Mom, she and my dad got out of the Air Force in 1972, and soon after, they moved to Fort Collins, Colorado, so that he could attend Colorado State. As she did while in the AF, my mom was a dental assistant, but my dad just wanted to party and wasn't very serious about school, so they moved to Bellingham, Washington for a fresh start and they had me.

Soon after, my mom met a man who painted eagles (who was the original focus of the story in 2004) and she had a few more friends, but only mentioned men. She described Puget Sound as beautiful, but her omission of girlfriends, when she really must have needed them, made me sad for her. My mom was still so resistant to divulging all the facts of her life when I was young, and she reminded me of a quote by Shelby Muhrin, "Love makes a fool of us all, darling." I laughed and I knew this to be true.

No one is immune to this. We have all been fools in love, and a woman with a baby who is dependent on her husband to support them is particularly susceptible to foolish love. This was a fact I knew all too well. In knowing a bit more of her truth, however scandalous it may be, it was clear that when I was a baby, my mom was doing the best she could for both of us. She was searching for stability that my dad couldn't give her. I truly believe in my heart of hearts, that she was doing the very best she could do as a twenty-six-year-old mother without mermaids to save her.

I prodded and asked her if she remembered anything more about when I was a baby. She had little more to tell me than what I already knew. I was born in the hospital in the summer of 1974. It was an easy birth and they brought me home, put me in a sling, and my mom went outside to pick blackberries by the river.

I realized that she likely recalled this joyous time in her life when I was a baby and that's why she wanted to go to the orchard when Ethan was fresh and new. It had been a full circle moment for her. According to my mom, sometime that year, she fell in love with another man and wanted a separation from my dad. Mom and her new man (and I) lived together for about a year. We lived modestly, but we were safe, and we were one with nature. I ate only oats and breast milk for the first year of my life, and I cut my first tooth on a high-ball glass at some older friends of hers who had a big house on the river.

But then, her boyfriend received a job offer to move to Alaska and work on the pipeline. It was too good an opportunity for him to pass up, and my mom released him out into the world to catch his brass ring. After that, Mom decided to go back home. Her father drove fourteen-hundred miles from South Dakota, to pick us up. We lived with my grandparents for a couple of weeks and then my mom found an apartment in a nearby town.

I spent my second Christmas with my mom in that apartment, and I am sure that my grandparents were thrilled to have their daughter and their first-born grandchild close and safe. I have no memories of my grandmother on my mom's side, as she died the following year, but she knew me, and I know that she loved me.

In the spring of 1976, my mom and dad decided to give wedded bliss another try, so my dad and his father drove from Colorado to South Dakota to pick us up. Our small and fragile family moved back to my dad's hometown of Craig, Colorado, and we lived across the street from my grandparents. Our house was a quaint white Victorian with dark green trim and shutters. I played at the same park my dad and his brothers had a generation before, and for a while, all was right in the world. When we were in our house on Lincoln Street, we were safe. Everyone knew what was going on, and Grandma and Grandpa were right across the street. I remember being a little girl in that quaint Victorian and going across the street for frequent visits.

This all made sense after my mom, and I spoke. I was caught up. I had my truth, and I could go on... but was I really? My dad loves me and perhaps I should extend him the same courtesy. So, now for a fork in the road. When I asked my husband if I should interview my dad too about his side of the story from 1970-1975, he said, "Shannon, come on. You are a journalist, and you know just as well as I do that there are three sides to every story: yours, mine, and the truth," The daughter in me was scared to ask but the journalist inside me wanted the other perspective, so that I could get closer to what happened. I believe now that each of us has our version of the truth and in the end, no one needs to be right. We just all need to be heard.

The way my dad remembered things after he and my mom got married, was a little different. The couple would serve another two years in the Air Force at Fairchild and finish their enlistments at the same time. They were married and the military wanted to ensure their launch into the real world was made successfully, together. The young couple decided to move to Fort Collins, Colorado so that Dad could go to Colorado State and earn his business degree on the GI Bill.

In the fall of 1972, they moved into a duplex on the corner of Meldrum and Mulberry streets only three blocks from campus. Three women lived in the unit next door. "They were wild as cut pears and the first time I ever heard 'Jesus, F@#&ing Christ,' was from one of those women." Dad continued about their time in Fort Collins, "I didn't really like school, and I wasn't going to classes, and when the VA found out, they stopped paying me."

So, the couple pivoted, and both went back to work. My mom worked as a dental assistant, as she had in the military, and my dad made a trip to the labor union hall. When I asked him what that meant he explained, "I gave them one hundred dollars to register and the next day I would show up and be guaranteed work and whatever they wanted me to do each day, I would do it, but mostly I would shovel." I asked him what he did then, and he said, "Shovel some more, and some more, and some more."

The young couple only had one car, so my dad would usually bike to work. After about a year of shoveling, he was promoted to driving a dump truck for about a week. After his stint in construction, Dad got a job as a tree trimmer's assistant. He told me about a time when he was standing on top of a pile of tree limbs while the tree trimmer was in the tree wielding his chainsaw. It was Dad's job to control where the debris landed. Before he knew it, the pile was twelve feet high, and he lost his balance. Alarmed by seeing my dad fall, his friend threw his chainsaw to the ground and ran around to the side of the house expecting to find my dad seriously injured or dead. But miraculously, he was all right. Somehow, he had fallen backward, flipped mid-air, landed on his feet, and was completely unscathed!

Things were not easy for the couple, but they were making an honest go of it. About this time, Dad said that he had been getting letters from a friend who lived back in Washington and described the area he had discovered as, "A gorgeous place, close to the water. There are a lot of companies hiring, berries grow on all the bushes, and it never snows." His friend encouraged, "It is paradise here. You have just got to come." So, in 1973 they moved to Puget Sound, and they were not disappointed by what they found. It was everything they had been promised and more. The young couple was ecstatic about their new opportunity.

They found a house about thirty minutes from town and just behind the house were two huge chicken farms with a combined capacity of raising twenty thousand chickens. Dad found work there sweeping out the chicken coops until he could find something better. Soon he got a job for the Department of Natural Resources as a member of a clean-up crew on prescribed burns. He was finally making decent money and the couple was happy meeting new people from his job. "But what did you do?" I asked. "Well, honey, we were mostly walking around with a five-gallon tank of water to snuff out any burning spots that were still active.

He recounted one fateful day when a fire started on the other side of the mountain, and they told my dad and his coworker to run up the hill to try to put it out. "We ran up the hill and tried to shovel dirt to put the fire out, but it was no use. When the guy I was with, who was making seventy thousand a year, ran the other way, I figured I better do that too. I was only making ten dollars an hour, and it was not worth my life."

My dad continued working for the Department of Natural Resources over the summer and in the fall, a new opportunity presented itself. He would work in a shake mill, which Dad described as a wood mill that cuts boards into cedar shakes that are 12-20 inches long. These rectangles are overlapped to create siding for the exterior of a house. He went on to explain that the shake mill was built from an old farm that a guy they knew had made into a mill. The owner would stand on the second floor of an open-air structure and feed twelve-foot boards through a huge blade. The shakes were cut, and gravity would send them down a steep ramp where Dad would sort the larger shakes from the smaller ones and package them accordingly. “Those shakes came down the shoot fast, but I could keep up. I got good at it and could pack a bundle in about thirty seconds.”

After all the calamities and dangers he had experienced at his other jobs, I sighed with relief. “So, it seems like compared to your jobs, this one was pretty safe. No trees to fall out of or fires to run from, right?” He laughed. “No, honey, this job was the most dangerous one of them all and let me tell you why. My boss would load the boards repeatedly with a lot of predictability, but sometimes the twelve-foot blade would get dull, and stick, and then it would break. It would sound like a bolt of thunder, and you knew to jump out of the way, fast.”

One memorable afternoon when he was packaging shakes the blade broke, thudded, banged, and went flying. No one was hurt that day, but it was a narrow escape and the blade landed two inches deep into a piece of lumber. “It could have cut a man in half. After that, my boss took us back to the office. We sat there in silence, and then he said, ‘It’s time to get back to work. Sitting around here worrying isn’t going to pay the bills.’” My dad continued to work at the shake mill despite the dangers and he swept the coops when they needed him.

In January of 1974, they learned that my mom was pregnant with me, which put extra pressure on them both, so they tried to make their own shakes for extra money. On August tenth, the shake mill was robbed overnight despite there being two Dobermans standing guard. The thieves had stolen about four thousand dollars' worth of cedar shake bails. So, the following night the boss asked my dad to park his 1969 International Harvester pick-up truck at the mill to keep an eye on the place.

He agreed to the plan because there was some extra money in it for him, but he told his boss that he was not going to leave his very pregnant wife home alone. So, they planned to spend the night in the back of the vehicle, parked at the mill. Having a vehicle there in plain sight, along with the dogs' presence, should be enough to keep the thieves from coming back. "We got to the mill around dark, and I made my rounds to check on everything. When I got back to the vehicle your mom said, 'It's time,' so we drove to the hospital in Bellingham, and you were born."

The love story of my mom and dad was vastly different than my own with Elijah, so comparing them left my head spinning. I am a romantic at heart, so obviously those were the stories that I initially connected with, but after imagining my mom and dad in the military, getting out, struggling to find jobs and make a living, I pondered what lessons I could learn from comparing my professional journey with theirs.

In 1970 the Occupational Safety and Health Administration was signed into law because people were being killed and maimed at work. My father gave several examples of what it was like to work without safety regulations that govern safety. My uncles and grandfather saw men die under railroad cars or heavy equipment while working in the coal mines as early as 1949. There certainly were no safety standards at the farm my grandfather was raised on, back in Kansas before moving to Colorado, and our country certainly paid a price for it. In the House,

Representative William A. Steiger worked for the passage of a bill. "In the last 25 years, more than 400,000 Americans were killed by work-related accidents and disease, and close to 50 million more suffered disabling injuries on the job. Not only has this resulted in incalculable pain and suffering for workers and their families, but such injuries have cost billions of dollars in lost wages and production."[5]

As a country of hard-working and competitive individuals, we needed OSHA then and we still need it today. We take it for granted that safety briefings, equipment, and policies protect our bodies and our rights as American workers, but I wonder if OSHA has failed to protect the American worker's psyche? There seems to be no governing body in our society that cares if an employee's mental health is respected, and we are now seeing the effects of that oversight.

The current state of the American workforce is highly disenchanted with an average turnover rate across all industries at 47%. Quiet quitting has become the new norm at many companies and the gig economy is where younger workers prefer to work. A 2022 Goldman Sachs survey found that 91% of small business owners already struggle with the current economy's impact on their industries, and 56% say the situation has worsened since 2022, painting a bleaker picture for the coming months and years.[6]

---

5 *OSHA. (2019). Occupational Safety and Health Administration. Retrieved February 3, 2024, from Osha.gov website: https://www.osha.gov/.*

6 *Blasbalg, C. L. (2022, November 24). 7 Small Business Challenges Owners Will Face in 2023. Retrieved February 3, 2024, from Wix Blog website: https://www.wix.com/blog/small-business-challenges.*

Not to be a total killjoy... let me assure you that with each generation, we do make improvements to our culture and the workplace is a huge part of our life, so it deserves our attention. In my parent's generation, OSHA was founded. What legacy will my generation give our children? What is needed is organizational leadership reform. But what that looks like is still up in the air since the global COVID-19 pandemic. We are once again rewriting what it means to live and work in a global economy and as American workers.

The statistics point toward a revolution or at least a reawakening, as Millennials resist the way things have always been done, and enlightened employees draw comparisons between European work-life balance policies and strategies and our own. It is clear that regarding work-life balance and workplace mental health, something has got to give.

After interviewing my parents, I discovered that my dad wasn't perfect. Neither was my mom. They both did the best they could do as young people in the 1970s and what more could anyone have asked of either of them? My sister was born in the summer of 1977 in the upstairs bathroom tub of our white and green Victorian. A doula and a friend attended the birth. My dad was a smoker, so to thwart his craving for nicotine he ate green onions dipped in blue cheese salad dressing. My sister was born into a happy family and her umbilical cord was tied with a shoelace. It was all a very neat affair, and I remembered those stories because they were told. My sister and I could talk about them and laugh.

I started visiting my paternal grandparents each day as soon as I knew my left from right. Their house was the place where everything was always tidy and fresh, and I was happy to be the center of attention. It was the best place in the world to me, and they had jellybeans. I have vivid memories of watching *Days of Our Lives* and *Little House on the Prairie* with my grandma.

I remember lots of other random things too, such as how she would wash and dry her paper towels so she could reuse them, chocolate cake, a plastic lemon squirt gun, performing songs along with Laurence Welk, and using my orange foam ball as the microphone, gravy on everything they ate, the smell of liverwurst sandwiches, laughter, my grandpa's garage and how he used to make lead fishing weights, all the elk and deer antlers in the garage, and her shaving his head each week with an electric razor that would often cut his scalp.

Grandma was very frugal. She knew how to stretch a dollar, put a good meal on the table, and afterward how to enjoy a good smoke and an entertaining TV show with her granddaughter on her lap. Contrastingly, and sadly, I do not have memories of my parents as a couple except one. I remember holding both their hands and walking in the dark two blocks away to the West Theatre to watch my first movie, Super Man. I've always looked at the few photos I have of the four of us together and tried to remember us as a family, but I have no solid memories of them ever being in love or even being in the same room. I was four and my sister was only one when the fairytale ended, and they officially divorced in 1978.

Now I had my story and I had learned about the journey and the challenges that my mom and dad had faced. These stories—the ones I already knew and the ones I learned while writing my book—define me as a human. I am glad that I had the time to finally pause and think about what I needed to learn from my family because the hard truth is that they won't be here forever and when they are gone, so are their stories, perspectives, opinions, and their wisdom.

I consider it criminal to consider that all this wisdom and love were nearly lost because I had gotten too busy to ask about it. Sometimes, looking back, asking questions, and letting powerful truths land in our hearts is necessary for healing, learning, and discovering what we want for our future. In my case, this practice has led to a new realization that my marketing career is over. I have learned so much over the years as I applied military principles to the civilian sector, and I take those lessons with me into this next chapter of my career as a scholar of organizational leadership.

Now, back to the love story... as my first husband and I started building a life in Spokane, I often thought about how it must have been for my parents. I romanticized their time there, but I knew very little of what life was like for them, and I suppose, at the end of the day, none of it really matters. They were stationed there for a few years, they worked hard and had fun. But it was the seventies and things were different for them. They obviously had challenges and they both did the best that they could. Through researching the details for *You Have Arrived*, I finally had a reason to ask the questions I had always wanted to ask but didn't.

My mother didn't like me prodding into her past, but she did tell me. My dad was more forthcoming with stories and details and for that I am thankful. I try to put myself in each of their shoes as you have hopefully tried to do as well. There is no blame on either side. It is just what happened. All of it; the love story and all the rest of it is ancient history, but it's part of my story too, and now I have claimed it.

Moving back home was a good fit for my parents, as it is for many young people who get out of the military. My mom and dad had support and if it wasn't for my grandmother's consistent presence and encouragement in my life, I would have become someone very different... less in many ways. My mom always considered my paternal grandmother to be her best friend. She loved her so much. So much so that she asked my grandma to be her maid of honor in her second wedding to my stepdad. "No, people just don't do that. I am your ex-mother-in-law. I can't be your maid of honor." "But" my mom pleaded, "You're my best friend and I want you to stand up there with me." So, she did.

Mom was light as a feather back then. She was a happy, content, sexy, thirty-four-year-old brunette, and there was nothing she couldn't do. On my mom and stepdad's wedding day in 1983, my little sister and I had flowers in our hair, cute blue and pink dresses, new shoes, and our grandma helping us get ready for the ceremony. It would be a simple wedding at the first church my sister and I had ever visited.

Everyone knew that as a child I had seasonal allergies, an inherited trait from my dad. I was, and always have been, a frequent and naturally loud sneezer. I even missed school a couple of times because my eyes swelled shut from hay fever. I remember that big old church was so stuffy. Between the pollen from the flowers, the dust in the old church, and the Charlie perfume that I had sprayed all over my dress in preparation for the big day, I started sneezing repeatedly in the minutes leading up to the vow exchange ceremony.

That day was the only time my grandma was ever cross with me. She pointed her finger at me, and I was taken aback. She was being stern. "Listen here, you cannot sneeze when we walk through those doors. You hold it in." I couldn't imagine how I could manage not to sneeze while in the middle of an allergy attack, but my grandma held my hand throughout the entire ceremony, and I didn't let go. I was so thankful for her on that day and for every day before and after that. Until I was thirty-two years old when she passed away, I had front-row tickets to see her in action. My grandma held her family and her community together until her dying day. She had a magical way of making everyone feel loved and even though you felt like you might implode, if she was there holding your hand, you would not.

Regarding the humanizing process of discovering my family's early history, I wonder what my employer could have done differently in the spring of 2023 to help me navigate the multifaceted stress of this time, so I didn't have to resign, because, in many ways, I did like my job as the director of marketing. But as I was approaching my forty-ninth birthday, I was exploring my life's purpose and the impact I would make on the world. In many ways, I was content with my life, but the past had been tugging at me for many reasons.

Now I know why. Because I worked remotely and never fully assimilated into a friend group while at work, I felt like an outsider. COVID-19 lockdowns in 2020 and the move to a new town only made it worse, as I felt I had no strong connections outside my own family in Florida. For a long time, I was alright with the five of us against the world, but not having other women to talk to took its toll on me.

I was still productive and passionate about my position with my company, and I was putting the hours in, but the level of negativity I was feeling was very high in the spring of 2023. I was serving my executive team, managers, and their subordinates each day and their disenchantment of our processes became my driving force. Everyone was complaining about things, but I was the one in charge of finding solutions. I wanted to help my company change and had found resources that would have made that possible. The revolving door or hires and fires was my proof that our company was broken, and no matter what I tried to do, I didn't have the authority to fix the issues.

My manager was the company's CEO and she rarely checked in with me. I felt like I was running her company for her and my efforts to improve it were never going to be enough, so I resigned. An organization with a healthier culture of inclusion and open communication that encouraged vacations and mental health would have saved me, and in learning these lessons, I know that I can never work for another company like this again and that is the pearl.

CHAPTER 4

OUR HAPPY HOME

Elijah and I had only been married six months when we moved to Spokane in December of 1995. We decided to live off-base, which meant a forty-five-minute commute, but after what had happened in the dorms at Castle—the level of control they have over you—we knew that living on-base was not our thing. We would happily make the drive to work each day if that meant we would preserve our freedom. We were so young and hopeful about life. The military paid to have our household goods shipped, so we drove with just the necessities from California to Washington in our Jeep Cherokee. Along for the ride was our two-year-old brindle boxer, Caesar, and our short-haired smoky gray tomcat, Hurray.

When we pulled into the driveway, the house seemed huge, and we felt lucky to have found it even though we had signed the lease sight unseen. The place was a gargantuan yellow, two-story Tudor with a large front porch, a full basement, a postage-stamp-sized backyard for our rowdy puppy, and five oddly shaped bedrooms, one of which was a second-story loft that took up the whole second floor.

Elijah was six-foot-three and even though he could only walk down the center of the room without hitting his head on the low vaulted ceiling, this spacious room with a view would be our love nest. Another negative feature of our bedroom was the old and quite repulsive, three-tone, royal blue, powder blue, and white shag carpet. I tried not to walk barefoot on it. As if these peculiarities of our bedroom were not enough, the literal icing on the cake was the white spackling that had been inexplicably stretched out into four-inch spikes in what can only be described as the home decorating style of eccentric masochism.

At first, the house seemed whimsical albeit odd, but after a few months of trying to do life there, its oddities made everything inconvenient. Admittedly, we both were struggling with the features of the rental, so we hatched a plan to buy our first home. Elijah and I both found second jobs, where we would work each night after our Air Force commitments, although we did decide to reserve weekends off to preserve our sanity. He and I were committed to our goal and at the end of that very long year we hoped it would be enough to pay off all our debt so that we could afford to buy our first home.

I donned an apron and became a server at Pan Handle Pies, while Elijah got a job as a nurse's aide at an Alzheimer's hospital, wearing turquoise scrubs. We would change out of our BDUs on the way to our second jobs that both started at six o'clock. We worked hard and sacrificed our evenings for a solid year until finally, in December of 1996, Elijah and I realized our dream of home ownership.

Elijah was an E-4 and I was just an E-3 but we were able to buy a three-bedroom, one-and-a-half bath house that was nineteen hundred square feet, plus a full basement for ninety-two thousand five hundred dollars. The house was in a good neighborhood and closer to work than our rental. It had two second-floor dormers and an exterior made of English brick with white trim. The sweet little house even had ivy cascading down from the eaves. It was perfect. I remember thinking when we bought the house that I couldn't wait to bring babies home here. We were going to have a wonderful life.

Built in 1942, with more than fifty years of life lived in its rooms, our little house had some oddities, including a few very odd paint choices, and layers of wallpaper representing each decade layered in the downstairs hallway. Whatever updates were required, we swore to do them. We painted and hung wallpaper, adding another layer to the hall, we laid carpet, planted new shrubs and flowers, built an arbor over the sidewalk near the street, and we even planted an aspen grove in the backyard. We loved that house, and it loved all of us right back.

We were good Airmen, and we liked a lot about military life, but in 1998, when we had our firstborn, things were already shifting. Andrew was born in January and after thirteen years as an ammo troop, Elijah decided to take an early out for a thousand dollars for each year that he had served. His first job after military life was at Pupo's Produce, and he was to be there just until he could find something better. To his credit, Elijah woke up at three o'clock, six days a week, and delivered produce and dairy products to restaurants and mom-and-pop grocery stores for about a year.

Thankfully, due to friends we met on base, over the next several years, I was eventually able to get him higher-paying jobs as a contractor. While Elijah got out of the Air Force right before our first son was born, I still had two years left of my second enlistment. After eight weeks of learning how to be a new mom, my maternity leave was up, and I was shocked to find my chair in the training room was now occupied by someone else.

I marched up the ramp to the squadron's personnel office and was directed back down the corridor to the mobility officer. He sat me down with some tough news. I had now been active duty for six years and most of the other Airmen in my squadron had gone on a remote by now. He advised me that the only way not to be sent away for a yearlong remote duty assignment to Saudi Arabia or Korea at this point in my career was to take a job outside of my squadron and join the Security Forces as their supply troop, which I eventually did.

I had an infant. I was finally a MOM. I was not leaving him. "But" he advised, "not going on a remote will kill your career." So, instead of leaving my baby boy for a year, I chose to kill my career. Easy decision. My final two years would be spent pumping milk each morning and afternoon and visiting Andrew at the Child Development Center at lunch. As a young mother in the military, I found the policies regarding family support to be more than fair and for the next two years, I would proudly serve the Supply and Security Forces Squadrons while balancing being a young mother.

Most days when I reported for duty I was excited about coming to work. I looked forward to being part of the mission, but after eight years of challenges and success in the Air Force, I was tired. I was ready to get out. They call it short itis, but I just absolutely and utterly loved being Andrew's Mom. I could not and would not leave him for one day, much less for one year, and I couldn't care less what I was giving up.

But there were things I loved about being in the military too, things I would miss, namely the camaraderie. As my last day of service approached, I started looking for something I could do that would fit well into my new life. Elijah and I were both aware that my being just a stay-at-home mom would not be enough for our checking account, or my social butterfly tendencies. I was due to get out on Valentine's Day 2000, so before I lost my relevance with my military connections, I started my Pampered Chef career.

That first holiday season, I poured myself into growing my business. For the next three years, I averaged two to three kitchen shows each week. I relished the friendships I made, the knowledge I shared, and the gratification I got from having permission to be the know-it-all in the room. When I got pregnant with our second son, Ryan in 2000, I just continued with my show schedule.

The pregnancy was easy, and my gig allowed me to take naps during the day when Andrew would sleep. When I had Pampered Chef shows in the evenings and on the weekends, Elijah would carry my tools to the van, and the husband of the party's hostess would haul them into their house for me. Although the Pampered Chef was not very lucrative, it did give me confidence and plenty of non-military friends, which was wonderful.

When I was very pregnant with Ryan, I can remember the one outfit that I could comfortably wear to perform cooking demonstrations. It was a lavender or black collared shirt under a heather gray tunic with straps and pockets. I had traded my BDUs for a new uniform and my new mission was to spread the important message of family mealtime. I was empowered and having fun, but I remember many nights being very pregnant driving around country roads with a printout of directions from my hostess' house without a cell phone or GPS, praying I would find my way home safely.

Somewhere between being an airman, a wife, a friend, and a mom, I decided to finally walk across the street to meet my neighbors. Carla was directly across from our house. She and her husband were members of The Church of Jesus Christ of Latter-day Saints, and they had an indiscriminate number of children. I could never figure out how many kids they had but the flow of people that went in and out of that little house reminded me of the business of an ant hill.

To the right of the Mormons lived Joann and Travis and their kids Rose and Richard who were a few years older than our boys. Joann and I, as well as Travis and Elijah, became fast friends and Joann taught me how to garden and make homemade humbaos (savory pork stuffed steamed buns) that tasted just like the ones she always ordered at Mee Sum at Pike Street Market.

To the left of the Mormons was a single lady named Connie, who looked to be about the same age as my mom. She had a black and white Shih Tzu named Mia. I knew the powder-puff's name because each morning Connie watered her flowers in her PJs while she talked on her cordless phone. Whenever Mia got too far away, she would stop talking on the phone and call Mia's name. "Mia, come. Miiiiiaaaaa, now!" Then, the little black and white pup would bound back to her mommy until she got distracted by a bug or the wind once more. Then the whole process would start again in about five minutes.

I liked to sit at my dining room table while feeding the boys and watch Connie and Mia. Soon after I was able to ascertain her character by peeking out my front window, she and I became friends. As was evident by her front lawn, night gown-clad morning strolls, Connie could care less about the opinions of others, and I loved that about her.

I began bringing over plates of food a few nights each week. Connie always seemed sad and tired, but she did better if the boys and I were there, so we found reasons to visit daily. Then in 2003, she was diagnosed with breast cancer. By then Connie and I were as close as neighbors a generation apart could be. I loved her and I wanted to help in whatever way I could in between taking care of the boys and work.

Despite us appearing to be a happy little family with two sweet boys, Elijah and I were having issues in the fall of 2003. There were broken promises all around me. There was also an alarming number of empty liquor bottles poorly hidden around our house. What was happening with my husband? As hard as Elijah would try to make me happy, he couldn't… so he would lie. I would discover his deceit and he would say, "I'm sorry," but nothing ever changed. He was indeed a sorry individual, and I loathed him for it.

To this day, the phrase, "I'm sorry," makes the hair on my neck stand straight up. There is just no reason for it if you do the right thing. Because of this perpetual cycle of disappointment, I didn't trust my husband… the father of our boys. To me, that meant that I couldn't love him, and I felt myself year after year, leaning on him less and withdrawing from our relationship. I started to look for apartments for me and the boys and soon realized there would be no way I could afford to leave Elijah with my current skill set and two little boys.

Our cute little house started to feel like a prison to me. But going across the street to Connie's every afternoon became my sanctuary and she, my greatest confidant. I thought that I had normal expectations of my husband; be honest, work hard, bring home your paycheck, and let your wife know where you are in-between. But these were things he was incapable of.

One night, Elijah had the grandiose notion he could easily make some fun money for himself at the casino on the way home from work. In a few hours, he had gambled away his entire paycheck and drained our checking account, but he didn't tell me, so a few days later when the mortgage, our phone bill, electricity bill, and car payments were supposed to clear the bank, they all bounced instead. Upon learning about this expensive mistake, I called the bank. Then Elijah finally told me what he had done… and he said, "I'm sorry."

I was done. I called his parents in Idaho Falls and told them about the situation. Since Elijah was too embarrassed to speak to them, I had to ask them for money to keep our family afloat. After I got off the phone with Elijah's parents, I asked him to move out. He left with his tail between his legs and then came home the next morning with a bad cold. Because of his foolishness, we didn't have a dime to our name, so he had spent the night at the river in his car. The next morning, Elijah was sad and apologetic, and like always, I let him back into our bed, and he swore he would do better. I didn't believe him. I was his doormat, again.

That was the day that Ethan was conceived. About two weeks later, we were fighting again about his lies, and by now, I had contracted his virus. I could feel my temperature rising and the deep itch of each sneeze that came out of me. I almost told him to leave again. "I don't give a damn where you stay but you are not taking Caesar this time!" The phone rang and to my surprise, it was my aunt from Colorado, who was visiting her mom who happened to be summering in Spokane with a friend. She and my uncle wanted to pop over for a visit and to see our house for the first time. Hearing her voice that day, at that moment, was as if someone had thrown me a lifeline, but this was a bad day. "Of course, you can come over," I replied, and they arrived about thirty minutes later.

My beloved aunt and uncle had no idea that Elijah and I were struggling so much or that I was so sick. After they left, I asked Elijah to go to the pharmacy and buy cough syrup and a pregnancy test. I felt so sick that I took the medicine first, despite the warnings against taking cold medicine during pregnancy, and then I peed on the stick. It was positive. There would be another baby to provide for, and I was locked in for another round of playing house. The next July 13th, Ethan Daniel, our little rock star was born.

Regarding the eighteen years I spent with Elijah, I realized that I did not love and lose. Instead, I loved and learned. After going through the madness that led to the end of our marriage, I became stronger. By loving a wonderful man who was also an alcoholic, I discovered that I no longer possess the capacity to process drama. I made a vow to myself when Elijah and I divorced that I would never ignore my small, quiet voice again and sacrifice my sanity in the process. A part of me knew that Elijah and I would end in a divorce when I married him, but I went through with it on that gorgeous morning on July 4, 1992, because my spirit knew that I needed to learn the lessons that he was going to teach me, and my heart knew that my boys had to be born into that union to be the men they have become. Also, perhaps, I had to go through all of this so that I could write it down and help you.

Elijah and I have gone through a lot and our relationship went from wonderful, to good, to intolerable for many years, then one day, not so long ago, he stopped drinking. For many years I believed that he was a pathological liar and that he was just born without a conscience, a psychopath. But I realized, very recently, that this is what alcoholics do... they lie.

Elijah and other alcoholics cannot have just one, or two, or even three drinks, and because of this his mind, body, and soul were in constant peril. I wanted to tell you our story, which is also his story because he and I both believe it will help others. So here is his side of the story.

EMAIL FROM ELIJAH: SUNDAY, JULY 9, 2023

The first time I drank and felt the effects was when I was sixteen. The alcohol transformed me into everything I wanted to be. I was so very shy and awkward. Sure, I was a soccer star and had friends, but it allowed me to talk to girls. Hormones were going rapidly at this time. I was in love with alcohol. This is where it all started.

I am not going to go into the depths of how it made me feel and what was missing deep inside me. What I can tell you is that by nineteen I was an alcoholic in every form. I did everything in the world to hide my drinking and would tell lies to keep it alive. I went through two outpatient programs and an in-patient alcohol rehab program when I was in the Air Force.

I was forced to not drink, (or be kicked out of the military) so I didn't. I also knew, deep down, that someday soon I would get to drink again. I have destroyed relationships and sucked the life out of the people I have loved. I could not take care of myself and didn't know how to. I knew how to lie though. That was easy for me. It's hard to explain, but I lied to keep my love of alcohol alive. But it was much more. I knew right from wrong. I wanted so hard to be accepted and I was a people pleaser.

When I knew that I did something that would disappoint someone in my life, it was easy for me to lie to save that pain. My brain was not capable of looking ahead and imagining what damage that lie would cause when I was found out.

Addiction changes the way a person thinks and their behavior changes. The guilt and trauma consumed me and so did the alcohol. I would do anything to numb my soul and forget about the bad things I had done. The best years of my life were taken from me. It took my children, my wife, my friends, my career, my health, my dignity, my purpose... everything.

Now how to overcome; well, you cannot, at least not by yourself. I was so proud for so long and did not want to ask for help, but then I did, and I have realized that I can never drink again, and remarkably I am okay with that. I know that now and I cannot change the fact that I hurt people that I love. I cannot get a lot of things back, but what I can do is grow in my spirituality. I cannot fix myself, no person, place, or thing can. Only GOD can do this. I cannot and will not live in the past. Doing so never lets you grow because you get stuck there and you can't see the goodness in the present. I also cannot think too much about the future, especially at the beginning of my sobriety journey.

Over-planning overwhelmed me. I felt I would not be able to meet the expectations others had of me. Now, I have goals, but to achieve them I live one day at a time. I try to learn from every day, and I try not to be too hard on myself. I wake up, connect with God, and thank him for another morning. Then I ask God to remove my shortcomings to keep me positive and fill me with the Holy Spirit. I have learned the best way to say, "I'm sorry," to all of those that I have hurt is by living my life and doing right by God. Hell, my words don't mean shit. Not really.

I now have a purpose in my life, and I have realized that before, when I was imprisoned by alcohol, I never had one. I also try so hard to just be positive, no matter what. I did and always will love you. Please don't ever think I didn't. Enough for now. Got stuff to do. —Sent from my iPhone

CHAPTER 5

THE GIFT OF THE NERVOUS BREAKDOWN

So, here I was, the mom of three little boys, and Connie, a divorcee' with a cute little dog, and two grown kids who didn't live with her. What could we possibly learn from one another? The answer was everything. Two weeks after Ethan was born, I registered for online classes at the University of Phoenix to earn my bachelor's degree in marketing.

Over the next two years, Connie and I leaned on one another hard. I loved her positive attitude and our long philosophical conversations. As if the physical drain of chemo and daily radiation treatments, as well as the realization of her mortality were not enough to put her anxiety into hyperdrive, Connie was also dealing with potentially losing her job at a large hospital cooperative in the region.

Her boss refused to change her job location, which was a busy pharmacy. Her doctor strongly advised Connie against being around people as much as possible. So, instead, she did the only thing she could do to protect herself; she would wear a mask. When customers asked why she was wearing one, she told them, "Because I have cancer and I am immunocompromised," which was the (ugly) truth that the organization didn't want to be part of their story. She got a reputation as a troublemaker.

Although there were available jobs that Connie could have been transferred into at the corporate office, the HR department refused to make reasonable accommodations to protect her. It wasn't until she threatened legal action that they reassigned her to a safer location. Throughout her treatment in 2003 and 2004, Connie masked up, held her head high, and went to work every day with integrity, while I did the best I could to support her with plates of pasta, glasses of wine, and an endless supply of empathy.

I also became her de facto IT person, although I was sorely unqualified for the role. I did the best I could do by helping her learn how to use her computer. I tried to explain what a domain name was while Connie vented about work. Due to my lack of any real employment in the civilian sector, I was unaware of the plights of the modern civilian workforce. Could they actually fire her for having cancer? They were making her so miserable that it seemed the company wanted her to quit... but the two of us had a plan.

Via the worldwide web, and the power of Firefox, Connie and I were going to find out what rights she had. We made it our mission to get her computer and internet set up so she could be empowered. When she turned fifty-five, Connie was thankfully in remission, and I had a new baby. She no longer had to wear a wig because her hair had started growing back. My beautiful friend now rocked a cute gray pixie style. The radiation treatments left her breasts black and sore. She assured me it was safe for me to lay Ethan on her chest as a comfort to her.

His sweet little onesie-clad body asleep on Connie's chest was a precious sight to me. She and I would often sit in her house or on her back patio under her big black walnut and chestnut trees and talk about the issues of the day or tales of the past, the latter always being my preference. After the baby was done nursing, I would always lie him on her chest for a nap, and Connie could breathe a little easier. I loved her and wanted to help, and the truth of the matter is that I really enjoyed spending time with her. I had three little boys and my mom lived in Colorado. I needed a maternal figure in my life... and she seemed to need me too.

To celebrate her birthday, the boys and I baked her a chocolate birthday cake, adorned with caramel ribbons and fresh edible flowers. We proudly brought the cake to her house as a surprise. She held the baby, and the boys were allowed to use her best China. She closed her eyes and smiled after taking each bite of her cake, wearing a paper birthday hat the boys had made for her.

Whenever we were together, Connie and I would have inspired and almost ethereal conversations. We laughed a lot, always, and her birthday was no exception as we lounged on the patio behind her house under the big trees. Ethan snoozed on her chest, and the boys played with their toy cars in her driveway. We laughed, had a glass of wine, and the baby just kept sleeping. That was the day that Connie told me about her nervous breakdown.

At the time of her exit from reality, she was a young mother with a baby and a toddler just fourteen months apart. She had a conservative Italian husband who was a stressed business owner, and his family did not approve of his choice of a wife. My sweet friend didn't go into much detail about the circumstances that led to her breakdown, and subsequent divorce, but it was clear that Connie and her husband had many struggles. There was also some domestic violence.

On that day while we chatted in her backyard, Connie told me about the time that she abruptly left her husband with her children. She went to go see her parents in Idaho for two weeks and the doctor prescribed medication and told her that she had a nervous breakdown from all the stressors she was dealing with. He prescribed rest so that she could regroup.

The important thing here is that Connie knew she needed help, and she sought it out. That help is okay in whatever it looks like for everyone. Labels don't really matter. It is all fine. You be, you, boo! Find and ask for help. Have the nervous breakdown or whatever you choose to call it. Connie, God Bless her, had the good sense to have hers., I want you to know that there is no shame in seeking a break from any aspects of your life that are too much. As long as you (and your kids) are in a safe place, take a break. You weren't meant to handle all the things that have been on your plate. Sometimes it all gets to be too much and you deserve and need a break.

Sadly, this would not be Connie's last nervous breakdown. Life is not easy for any of us and after beating breast cancer, Connie would have some other really hard battles to fight. But she has always been good at taking time to pause, regroup, rally her mermaids, rebuild her life, and somehow, miraculously find joy again. I had forgotten about the wisdom that can be found in having a nervous breakdown, but by reconnecting with and recalling the time spent with my sweet neighbor, I realized that a break was exactly what I needed.

CHAPTER 6

EMBRACED AT MOUNT OF OLIVES

In many ways, life was wonderful in Spokane (except I was raising children with a liar, and I couldn't do anything about it). Our extended families were both scattered throughout Colorado and Idaho and living in Washington kept us close (enough) to them. We had developed so many wonderful and supportive friends in Spokane and we even had a weekend lake cabin. *Would a change in our environment change Elijah? In my naivety, I thought perhaps that it would.* The practical argument for relocating was that after so many failed attempts at Elijah finding a good job and us both working opposite shifts to save on daycare, our quality of life financially could use some improvement.

So, in the summer of 2005, we moved our three little boys across the U.S. from Washington State to Panama City, Florida, so Elijah could pursue his career as a military contractor, and I could finish my marketing degree without so much financial stress. It was the ultimate adventure and dice roll in life and I prayed that the huge move would be good for our family. I secretly hoped that Elijah might stop drinking and lying so much, and I thought that if we were away from everyone who knew and loved us, we could focus on just us... he would only be accountable to me and his boss. Certainly, Elijah could handle that. And if it all went to shit, at least we would be in Florida, and isn't everything more beautiful in the Sunshine State... even divorce? *Hope for the best but prepare for the worst.*

At first, our gamble seemed to pay off. We took Panama City by storm as a beautiful young couple with three little boys. Elijah had a lucrative and rewarding career that he loved, and I became a praise and worship leader at a large Baptist church on the beach. But, as time went on, despite having great friends, a loving church family, a good job, and a house with a pool, my husband's lies just got more and more frequent.

In 2010, as much as I loathed becoming a divorce statistic, I could no longer breathe. The family that the five us had been fell apart in the face of mistrust and alcoholism and I could no longer hold it all together. I had become a doormat, and I was angry all the time about it. Elijah and I were constantly short with one another and although I begged him to change, he kept on lying.

This was the first time my sanity was tested, although I did not call it a nervous breakdown or a midlife crisis, because, frankly, Americans just don't have those anymore. There are exceptions to this rule that we all recognize, such as a man who is going through a midlife crisis will buy the stereotypical red sports car, whilst trading in his wife for a younger model. But let's get real, mid-life crises are looked at as hiccups that silly balding men have. Mental health is riddled with misconceptions, denial, over-medication, social mores, and insensitivities.

The terrible result of the American grind is that every eleven minutes someone commits suicide in the United States and over the past twenty years 87% of those who commit suicide are men.[7] But most women don't have the luxury of having a

7 *Centers for Disease Control and Prevention. (2021, March 25). Fast Facts. Retrieved February 3, 2024, from www.cdc.gov web-*

mid-life crisis, or a nervous breakdown, and most of us don't commit suicide because we have children, and we are the moms.

Take stock of the women around you. You know that it's true that most American women are medicated, tired, disillusioned, undervalued, and overworked. In the vast majority of homes and offices, women do the lion's share of the work, and because women make less only 82% of what men earn—and because women always put others first—many women never take vacations.[8] This disparity between gender work distribution and fewer opportunities for females to rest is a sad paradox that has been a part of American culture since its inception. So, we just do the best we can and have our nervous breakdowns in private.

What would the neighbors think... even worse, what would the judging eyes of Facebook think when they saw their friend go unhinged on social media? What would they think about her frequent trips to visit girlfriends or the memes she was posting embracing the great resignation? What would they think of her now; especially since they knew how much she loathed Trump? Would they think she sold out when she just stopped caring about her friends' and family members' political affiliation? What would everyone think when she just decided to love them anyway? What would the judges and juries in my midst think when they discovered that she quit my job after her husband was diagnosed with cancer? Would they assume she was having a nervous breakdown, or a mid-life crisis, or would friends and family just abandon her and say, "She has always been crazy, but

site: https://www.cdc.gov/suicide/facts/

8 *Aragão, C. (2023, March 21). Gender Pay Gap in U.S. Hasn't Changed Much in Two Decades. Retrieved February 3, 2024, from Pew Research Center website: https://www.pewresearch.org/short-reads/2023/03/01/gender-pay-gap-facts*

lately she just became a giant bitch, and you know what, she is a bad wife."

Would they understand why I made these decisions? By now you probably recognize that the hypothetical questions in the above paragraph are questions I asked myself shortly after my husband was diagnosed with cancer. Oftentimes, when big life events hit, we must reevaluate and reassess our lives and take a step back from what is happening.

It felt liberating to do it, but also scary. How much did I care what others thought of me? It turned out that I really did care what my husband's family thought of me. I felt their disapproval as if it were a weight on my chest, even from twelve hundred miles away. They didn't think I was being a supportive wife, and, in many ways, I wasn't, but my ability to breathe had become an issue. My high blood pressure escalated to panic attacks, and I lost the ability to put on a smile and endure the stress. I had to find new ways to depressurize. Making changes had become a matter of survival.

"Sometimes my walk looks strange, but it's that way for a reason... and I still have to walk it."

Me, 4-20-2023

It has been nearly six weeks since I have been able to circle back to Chapters four through thirteen. I now find it foolish that I once thought I had written this book in thirty days. Sure, I journaled 30,000 words, and I did put thoughts on paper for exactly a month, but that is not writing a book. Writing a book is a methodical labor of love. It is essentially making sure each word works to paint the correct picture for you, the reader. It's making sure thoughts are concise, and that these concepts will resonate.

I want to make a difference or what's the point of this exercise... besides catharsis?

Then, there is the researching and confirming of memories and validating claims about other people. Is the dirt I am putting on display necessary to help you to trust me? Will the revealing details that I plan on releasing out into the world ultimately be useful or helpful? Do the ends justify the means? Writing a book like this one is about making sure names can be used and fact-checking everything. Writing a book is different than journaling, but journaling can be the beginning of a book. I am proof of that. This process is exhausting and it's not fast, because writing a book like this cannot be rushed.

There are days that I don't get to my manuscript at all, and I start getting nervous and grouchy. The things of life sometimes pull me away from my manuscript and those days are discouraging. I want to honor this project and get it out as soon as possible, but it simply cannot be done quickly, within the constructs of living life. But I endure through fifteen versions, to the dismay of my editor who has long since lost her patience with me.

Out of complete desperation and humility, I sought counseling from the Godliest man I knew, the head pastor of our church. He asked me to write down why I was so angry because at that point I was unsure why. Things were so good in so many ways, but I was dead on the inside. After he read about the sham that was my marriage, he gave me the permission I needed after 18 years of living in chaos with an alcoholic. The dream of the happy little family was officially over, and the only way forward was to divorce the father of my three sons. It was and is one of the saddest things we have all had to endure.

When we lived in Panama City, those around us viewed my divorce from Elijah as a tragedy. Everyone at church said that "they would pray for our family." But no. Don't pray that we will make it. Please don't do that. It's already broken and now we must move on, the sanctity of a Godly marriage be damned.

I didn't want to be at church and felt like I had let so many people down and I quit the music program. I couldn't go through a divorce while I was leading praise and worship. Those two worlds did not coexist in my mind. I was confused and distraught, unsure, and challenged by what would be my new reality as a single mom raising three little boys with no family to help. I just wanted to feel safe and be loved by a man who could love and protect me and be honest about things. I wanted a man in my life I could count on and be proud of in any room.

Around that time, a special word kept coming out of my mouth. You know that word, "manifest," right? It's often used in the context of, "I am manifesting a new life that is going to be amazing." Most people around me thought that I was completely off my rocker. The truth of the matter was that I was letting my weird hang out, and I didn't care who witnessed it. I had run out of energy to fight with Elijah, and I was focused on doing what I knew was right for me and the boys. Their father had lied about everything and anything for years. Our marriage was a sham, and I was over it. I just wanted my sons not to turn out like their dad. One of his kind on the planet was enough and I considered it my civic duty to prevent Andrew, Ryan, and Ethan from turning out like their father.

My inhibitions were low, and the stakes were high as I contemplated my next move. Looking back, I know that the reason I was able to cope with the separation and divorce I had to file was because a man who owned a local health food store down the street from my house took pity on me. I had gone to Mount of Olives one Sunday afternoon, and truth be told, I was desperate for help in whatever way he could offer. Supplements are important. I have always taken them, but what I needed now was something better... something magical, if that even existed.

By now I had graduated with my marketing degree, and I was working for the local newspaper in ad sales. I was overwhelmed, unhealthy, and overweight, but still optimistic that there was a solution. I just wanted something to help me cope with the mountain of stress that was all around me. The fact was that at thirty-six years old, I was going to be single again, and soon. What did that even look like for me at this stage of my life? I had been with Elijah since I was eighteen and now, I was eighteen years older and wiser, with stretch marks and cellulite, but I wanted my independence more than anything. I wanted to feel pretty again.

I have been thinking a lot about body image and weight and how I want to express the truths I have learned about weight and self-worth. My mother has always been on a diet, so I think my obsession to lose weight before divorce was influenced by society and my mom. As it is for all of us, our body image plays a large role in how we see ourselves fitting in the world. The psychology of body image is complex and very personal, but your weight does not diminish your importance as a human or dull your sparkle as a complete child of God. It just doesn't.

Over the years, I have worried less about weight and more about health, and if someone loves you, they won't care about your weight. I have been thin, and I have been fat, and I can truly say that I have loved myself the same either way. This is the attribute that's what draws people into your fold, confidence. What I want to drive home to you right now is this... Love yourself. Be healthy physically and mentally. But please do not wait to step out and do the next big thing because you are not happy with what you see in the mirror. The world needs your contributions right now. Life is short and we are not guaranteed tomorrow.

Love yourself enough to be bold, no matter your dress size. If not now, when?

I was breaking my family. Could I handle the stress of raising the boys alone? Yes. I knew it would be less stressful than living with a liar. I would work as hard as I could to make sure that the boys' were provided for. I would insist that Elijah help support them and still be in their lives and be a good dad, at least as much as his alcoholism and dishonesty would allow. We would be good co-parents and we would both love and support our boys. That's what they deserved.

Around the time of my first major proverbial flush, I also recognized that I had been robbed of something precious while staying with Elijah, intimacy. I didn't feel safe with him and hadn't for many years. I had been doing my best to rationalize that all marriages have issues and that no one was perfect. Most men tell their wives little white lies now and then, right? And the most ridiculous advice that I had been given by my mother was, "Just be grateful for what you have." But, at this point, nothing was going to keep me in this marriage, I wasn't grateful for this situation, and I was done with feeling like a doormat.

A glimmer... I also had enough faith to know that I could find someone who would treat me better than him. I wasn't exactly afraid to be alone, but I knew that life is better when you are in love. I wanted a new man in my life to fill my heart and to also undue Elijah's negative influence over the boys, if that was even possible.

When we separated Elijah kept the boys almost every weekend. For the next three years, I would date men that I met online and explore the type of man I needed. I made some mistakes but learned so much more about the dynamics of a healthy relationship. My village of girlfriends, some going through their own divorces, became my sounding board. I had married so young and sowing my wild oats as an adult had a completely different set of rules.

I would be honest with the men I dated regarding my situation and my expectations of them. The prospect of dating at this stage in my life was as exhausting as it was exhilarating, but in truth, I didn't feel physically ready to take it on. I still looked like a chubby, uninspired housewife... someone else's wife and I rationalized that no one wanted to take that woman out to dinner. It was time to get down to my fighting weight. It's just how I felt about it at this point.

In my search for balance and health, I walked in the door to my favorite health food store, Mount of Olives, and saw Matt. The pleasant wave of eucalyptus and mint filled my lungs, just like always. He was stocking shelves in the back and welcomed me in. I liked Matt, but I think everyone did. He was young, handsome, soft-spoken, and muscular. He always spoke about how much he loved his store, how much satisfaction he found in helping his clients, and how much he adored his wife and little girl.

Matt and I had become familiar at this point as I had become a regular, buying supplements and salves for the boys' rashes from time to time. But this visit to his store was different and I think Matt sensed it. For one, I had no little gentleman holding my hand. I leveled with Matt. "I am at the end of my rope here, dude. My husband is a liar and I'm filing for divorce. What can you recommend for that?"

I thought he would laugh at my honesty or perhaps offer a reassuring hug. But no. Matt actually had something in mind for what ailed me. He turned around and walked down the first aisle, all the way to the left, to the very back of the store. He climbed a ladder and reached back behind another inconspicuous product to grab a blue container with a silver logo. I was surprised that he had something at all for me, and I wondered, "Why all the cloak and dagger?" Matt explained that the contents of the blue container were in fact legal and that this was *the good stuff.*

Matt explained that Somatomax was a synthetic human growth hormone supplement that he had been taking for the last twelve months. Matt assured me that there were no serious side effects reported and it had been on the market for several years. This powder that looked and tasted like Kool-Aid enabled his clients and him to lose weight, sleep better, and build muscle tone, and it even produced a feeling of euphoria. "Sign me up for THAT, Matt."

I gave Matt a high five along with forty-seven dollars and started taking a scoop of the supplement in twenty-four ounces of water each night before bed. I told the boys that it was Mommy's special drink and that it was off-limits. Needless to say, the recommendations of someone who knew about supplements helped me get through my divorce, and it did help me lose weight, get healthy, and feel more confident at a very difficult stage in my life.

I was thankful that I had been brave enough—make that desperate enough—to ask Matt for help and more thankful that he had a solution for me. Taking health food store supplements, attending life-coaching sessions, going to church, and being supported by my village of girlfriends in Panama City helped me during my divorce, but, after a few months of dating the duds of the Florida Panhandle, I was tired and considering moving back to Colorado or Washington. But something was keeping us in Florida. I could still feel this place's pull on me, although I didn't know why.

Dating with kids is just tough. I found that if the men I met in Panama City already had children, everything was so complicated, and many of the men without children were not thrilled about the prospect of an insta-family. After a few horrible first dates and a couple of long-term failed relationships, I resolved that if the man I was with did not believe that my boys were the best part of being with me, they were simply not worth my time. This time around, I was not going to put up with dishonesty, anger, or nonsense.

I remember my deep introspection about my adult life when I was going through my divorce in 2010. I realized then, that during the decade that had led up to the separation I had been methodically but quietly taking steps that would lead me down the path to being single in Florida. The realization that those steps had taken me to where I was now standing overwhelmed me with emotion. I had been making semi-conscious choices all along to get me to where I was.

I encouraged Elijah to take the job in Panama City because in 2005 the small voice inside that had been whispering had begun to scream at me. "Break away or you will go mad! You can't be a good mom if you go crazy. Move to Florida. Get away from your friends and family. You can do it without them. Start your lives over again." I rationalized that in Florida I could see Elijah's intentions more clearly and that he may be a better husband there. Or maybe I would be able to see his truths and his lies more clearly in Florida. I wasn't sure... but I felt a strong Southernly pull, so we went.

Another important worst-case scenario step I took to prepare me for what I knew was to come, was to sign up for classes when Ethan was an infant in 2004. I was ready even though Andrew and Ryan were only six and three. I recognized that juggling the mom stuff, wife stuff, and nursing a baby while earning my degree would be a monumental challenge, but it was necessary. Because I had joined the Air Force right out of high school, and not gone to college, I felt like I was way behind the eight ball. I found a way to balance it all and my sons became my reason why. I committed to working harder than anyone else to earn my degree so that I could support them and set an example that even though things may be hard, they are not impossible.

I was taught by my amazing freshman Science teacher, Pete Bergman, that organization is the key to success. But being organized will only get you so far in life. One must also be educated. It's your passport to the future. I needed to get organized in my life, earn my degree, move to Florida, and do so many other small things to set myself up for what I knew would be my future in 2010 and beyond.

My first nervous breakdown certainly changed my life and my sons' forever, and I still don't know if the decisions I made in my early thirties were good for the boys or not. All three of them have grown into kind, intelligent, and sensible men, and I am proud of who they are. I recognize that moving them across the country and then divorcing their dad five years later certainly changed who they would become, but this was our path, and I knew I was a good mom.

At our house, there would always be love, laughter, games, a full refrigerator, and so many friends. I know that for me, living in Florida forced me to hustle. More importantly, divorcing Elijah gave me the confidence to push myself and be brave, both personally and professionally. One thing is for certain; I know that if we hadn't moved to Florida in 2005, I wouldn't have met my Amazing Man eight years later and life certainly looks different now because of that.

In my early thirties and again in my late thirties, and especially right now, I have realized that I can rise to the occasion when I am faced with challenges. Tony has dubbed me a "wrecking ball" and how fitting that nickname is, because just as a wrecking ball knocks down buildings so efficiently, so do I.

Here's my process: I compartmentalize my disdain and frustration, and I keep smiling for as long as I can, gathering energy. Then, I make a plan and only when the time is right, I knock all the barriers out of my way. It is really just phenomenal how things always seem to work out. I think that if I had to build a diorama that represented my life it would look like a psychedelic mountain of inverted and sideways-found utilitarian objects from a landfill that has been repurposed and put back together in odd ways that are as beautiful as they are absurd. Unicorns would frolic, mermaids would swim, and glitter would fall from the sky at all hours of the day and night. Oh, and I couldn't forget about the phoenix and how she can magically rise from the ashes. True to my alma mater, when necessary, I have become that phoenix! God just seems to honor my dysfunction and honesty. He holds my hand through it all and good things just fall into the right nooks and crannies. Looking back now, I can see that my life has been made better, not despite the fact that I am a wrecking ball, but because of it.

I planned my escape to Florida so far in advance and so perfectly before I imagined what I wanted from my life, and now it was happening. My conscious mind could not comprehend what was going to happen ten or fifteen years in the future, but the Universe in her infinite wisdom was guiding me to earn my degree, move to Florida, file for divorce, change jobs a lot, and earn the right to start my consulting firm and write this book that you are now holding.

Over the years, I have learned how to trust the chaos of my life and to just let the process happen. I hope that as I have aged and mellowed, I somehow look less neurotic to those around me during my episodes of drama, but I probably look just as ridiculous. What I have discovered is that when you honor the chaos, the boldness, the creativity, and the screams of the small voice inside, the universe will reward you. How could it not?

So yes, this is the story about thirty days of turmoil and other retrospection. During the thirty days I journaled I was leaving breadcrumbs for my later self. Over the past several months I have been filling in those blanks for you. We haven't even gotten to those fated thirty days yet and you already know me so well. The process to make You Have Arrived has been a lifelong project in the making. Years before my conscious mind could even comprehend what I was doing or why I was doing it I was preparing to connect with YOU at this exact time in YOUR life to help you process something hard that you are dealing with.

Sometimes we all need a little motivation to take the first step toward our arrival. What that looks like for you is up to you. But since I am also a second-generation Kansas-dust-bowl-farmer-type-of-hard-worker, I could not help but relinquish my whole heart in this process to be as transparent as possible. I have embraced this nervous breakdown, because there is no shame in it, and it has empowered my husband and I to renegotiate our priorities. You Have Arrived has become my best friend and a cathartic experience, releasing more than 30,000 words in thirty days as I traveled to see my mermaids and I let the waves wash over me, liberating me from the miserable constructs that I was accepting as my life.

As a marketer, I love good taglines. Don't we all? The neat little bow that we can tie around something to make it make sense is a comfort to us in so many ways. So, as you can probably guess, as I am coming out of this period in my life, I have adopted a new life mantra. It is blessedly simple and relates to all humans, no matter where they are in life, and it is just this; "If not NOW, when?"

"Another world is not only possible; she is on her way. On a quiet day I can hear her breathing."

— Arundhati Roy

CHAPTER 7

EQUILIBRIUM

When you are really, truly, and deeply in love with a man who is diagnosed with prostate cancer, it stops you in your tracks. To completely love someone is to love their body, soul, and mind in equal measure. That's what I promised in my wedding vows. So, when your husband's body is diagnosed and is being treated by doctors to save his life, you naturally must take care of his physical needs, but caring for his mind and soul is infinitesimally trickier.

I had to get real in the moment of diagnosis and I surmised that a prostate cancer diagnosis at fifty years old meant something very serious about the whole person I had loved and built my life around. His mind and his soul had sold his body a bad package of goods, and now he was suffering. I adore this workaholic and respect his desire to work hard, but things have been off balance for ten years.

My husband's life was now in jeopardy because of this imbalance and his diagnosis is bona fide proof that he has not taken care of himself, despite my constant pleading to go to the doctor, the dentist, the optometrist, and to eat better, drink less, work out more, as well as schedule regular check-ups. Our mental and soul health has been ignored for too long as well. The quantifier is that we haven't been on a vacation in the ten years we have been together because we have been raising boys and working hard. Vacations help you decompress but we don't do that.

Another reason vacations were overlooked is that we live in Florida, and our family usually comes to stay with us, and being good hosts, we would take time off. We only get ten days off a year, so it was used up quickly. Even though we both work constantly, over the years, I noticed that we just didn't have time or money to go on a vacation like everyone else. If we did take a day or two in conjunction with a weekend or over the holidays, our phones would always be close at hand. Texts, calls, and emails had to be answered because we were invaluable at work.

The result of the rat race that Tony and I have been in for the past ten years was that we never got the chance to unplug, relax, and recharge. We were on a hamster wheel, and it just never stopped, and the stress mounted. Stress causes cancer for God's sake, and it's proven. What were we doing to ourselves and to what end? Well, we discovered that the end was prostate cancer at fifty years old.

Tony has made providing for the family his priority instead of his health, and frankly, I hate him for it. Women get pedicures and visits with girlfriends, mammograms, and pap smears. Self-care is encouraged in our culture for women. But for most men who must provide for their families, self-care, even hanging out with friends, is considered a waste of time.

This disparity has infuriated me for so many years, and I know it is why my husband has cancer now. So, I can't just take care of his physical health… I have to make him start caring about himself for the first time in his life. I will plant my feet in the sand and say NO MORE. "I told you so," does not begin to encompass my feelings about this. I not only begged him to change his priorities. For years I have been begging him to just put himself on the list, but he refused. It's the only thing we ever fight about. And why now? We have been raising kids without the other parent participating for ten years. Tony didn't even want kids, but he stepped up to the plate and became the dad that our boys needed.

With invasive and toxic radiation scheduled to be injected into his prostate in the next few hours, putting himself on the list is still a foreign concept to him. He wants to resign from his job because he can't keep up with his workload. He's just too tired while on Androgen Deprivation Therapy (ADT), and although his employer is pretty understanding, my husband feels worthless and wants to quit his job and just give up. What is the point of trying to catch up at this point? He must be successful at work because that is how he defines himself and that is the problem. Ever since I have known Tony, he has been afraid to step away from his phone or desk for more than a day or two out of fear of failing at work and letting his colleagues and clients down. This is why he doesn't want to go on a vacation. I get it.

My last corporate job was the same way. These high-level executives in charge of their companies sit at the helm and run their ships without the slightest clue what their employees must do to keep their departments running. They enjoy the profits made from their employee's toil. They go on plenty of vacations. They have no problem unplugging because they have a net of diligent soldiers who are fearful of losing their job if they don't perform each day with the greatest sacrifice. Their dedicated soldiers are struggling to take a moment for themselves.

Especially after COVID-19, we all need to take a break and enjoy life a little bit. Isn't this what the pandemic taught us? We have lost over a million Americans to the pandemic; babies and mommas, the old, and the young, brothers and sisters who didn't deserve to get sick and die, but they did, and here we are, just falling back into our routines as a culture, working at our desks, going to the meetings, and teaching the classes, as if nothing happened.

Regardless of where they work many employees experience emotional exhaustion, anxiety, and depression due to work demands and these symptoms have been made worse by the pandemic. One estimate is that depression and anxiety disorders cost the global economy $1 trillion each year in lost productivity.[9]

The attitude of gratitude will only get you so far. You shouldn't just have the things you need to get by... you deserve the things you want too. So, how do we get there? First, if we don't have our health, we truly have nothing, so do everything mentally and physically you need to do to stay healthy, especially if you have made the choice to bring children into the world. They are counting on you to be around for a long time, so don't disappoint them.

Education about mental and physical health can be found anywhere but be sure you are getting your advice from a licensed professional, or at least a legitimate website. There has been so much misinformation spread about health and nutrition, so choose your resources wisely.

We must do better in this country and remember to live when we can, whatever that looks like to each of us. We won't be here forever, and our health is all that matters. For us, better mental health was complex, a list of over a dozen things we needed

9 *Chodavadia, P., Teo, I., Poremski, D., Fung, D. S. S., & Finkelstein, E. A. (2023). Prevalence and Economic Burden of Depression and Anxiety Symptoms Among Singaporean Adults: Results from a 2022 Web Panel. BMC Psychiatry, 23(1). https://doi.org/10.1186/s12888-023-04581-7*

to check off. But perhaps the most important thing was to seek knowledge.

We have already established that knowing your origin story is important. I was discovering on my own but Tony needed to do more than make a couple of phone calls to discover who he was. When Tony was eighteen and living in Florida, he came home to visit his family in Illinois. On the last night of his trip, his mom revealed that he was adopted by both his dad and his mom. The knowledge of the hidden adoption sent him into a disruptive tailspin for about a year. At that time, Tony attempted to find his birth parents and to discover the story that led to his conception, but the adoption was closed, so the state of Illinois could not release any information to him.

He let it go, went on with his life, and became resolved to the fact that he already had a big family who loved him. The names and faces of those other people who had conceived him were of little consequence. At least that is what he said whenever he would speak of his origin, but in the quiet, sometimes inebriated private conversations we had, Tony would sometimes tell me that he yearned to know why his birth parents gave him up. He once told me, "I must have been a real piece of shit, even as a baby, for them to just give me up," and even though we both knew that this was not true, a piece of him felt discarded, unwanted, and less loved than his four younger siblings who came from a loving couple's legitimate courtship and bond.

His rational mind could push these thoughts away, but I knew that someday to fully self-actualize, my husband would need to know the whole story of who he was and where he came from, no matter how scandalous that story might be. For his sanity and my own, and for him to smile as large as I knew he could, I encouraged him to order a DNA test. In January 2023 he finally agreed to it, primarily for the practical reason of knowing if his genetic markers put him at risk for other diseases.

But I know in his heart he yearned to discover his origin story just as much... maybe even more. We have all heard it on daytime talk shows and at our counselor's office; "If you can't love yourself, how can you expect anyone else to love you?" I believe this with my whole heart, and I felt that Tony needed to know his story to evolve. If not now, when? This block was preventing him from fully experiencing joy and fully showing up for himself.

When you don't love yourself enough to ask for help, no help will be given. Even if help is offered, because you can't love yourself, you won't accept it. This is where we were at, and I was tired of him not liking himself. I was afraid of what might happen to us if he didn't move past this block.

The DNA test had gone unused for over a month, and I knew Tony was afraid to take the test. He was procrastinating but we weren't talking about it. This was what I wanted the topic of conversation to be on the way home from Moffitt Cancer Center after his Brachytherapy. I purposely chose a significant conversation after his procedure, as I felt like today would be a pinnacle of physical and emotional health. My "doer brain" was ready to move on to the next thing. But as I drove my husband home from the hospital that day, I soon realized that there would be no substantial conversations.

To prepare for Brachytherapy, an outpatient procedure, my husband was required to fast for two days. The procedure had gone as planned and after he woke up, he felt a little woozy. His prostate gland had been injected with active radiation by sixteen needles, so the catheter was left in to allow the swelling to go down. He was full of painkillers, and he felt horrible, obviously. He was white knuckling the dashboard trying to hold onto his constitution as I navigated the roundabout and tree-lined streets outside of the hospital.

We were both relieved to be leaving the hospital. It felt nearly celebratory, and I began talking to him about the unused DNA test. That's when he turned green. "You have got to pull over, babe," he said. I turned into a Burger King parking lot where he opened the door and threw up the water that was in his stomach. I knew food would help, so I parked by the entrance and then ran to get him something. I came back to the car with a blue Power Aid, a small Whopper, chicken fries, and French fries. He didn't want any of it, but I encouraged him to get something in his stomach.

He was still feeling horrible, and nothing sounded good, but he ate a few fries and drank some Power Aid, and soon the dry heaves stopped. It was a relief to know he was feeling better, so we chit-chatted about what was in front of us; a nothing conversation. The topic was the over-processed and salty food that we both found repulsive. Our family rarely eats fast food and we had forgotten how bad it was. I tried to get his mind off of how miserable he felt, and we talked about how tragic it was that so many people live off fast food because it's fast and cheap, but devoid of nutrition.

His nausea and the clinical reality of his treatment certainly changed the topic of conversation as we drove the thirty minutes home across the bridge into Clearwater. I wanted to talk about things we needed to do next to move forward, but he could barely handle a short car ride. It was on the way home from the hospital that day that I first felt like a caregiver. I despised the word they use to refer to the spouses of the person who is sick. My husband wasn't that sick. He was still fine and working, and we were going to kick cancer's ass. We had a good plan medically and no chemotherapy was necessary to beat his prostate cancer, and he certainly didn't need me to be his "caregiver." He wasn't that sick… but today he was, and he needed a caregiver, and that person was me.

When we got home, Tony was spent. I helped him into the house, hung up his catheter tubing and bag on a chair next to our bed, tucked him in, and closed the bedroom door. I breathed a sigh of relief and broke down into tears and ran outside to breathe in the fresh air. That's when I saw a stream of pungent liquid running down the street and a huge pool of oil under my car. I could only surmise that the oil change I had gotten a month prior had been faulty and it was on this day, of all days, that my husband could not physically help me that the oil pan cap decided to come dislodged. The timing of this environmental disaster was not lost on me. I broke down in tears again, shaking my fists at God, then regrouped, and set to cleaning it up with my son and a couple of caring neighbors. I had resisted the label of caregiver, but that is what I was, like it or not.

At any one time, about 12% of the population are considered caregivers in the U.S. and the stress they deal with, even if they don't show it, is significant.[10] Caregivers report experiencing anxiety, depression, and substance abuse five times more frequently than non-caregivers, and six percent of caregivers resign from their jobs from burnout like I did. The American Psychiatric Association offers education and resources for employers who want to do a better job of supporting their employees who find themselves in the caregiver role. Creating a more caring culture around caregiving is the key.[11]

---

10 *DeAngelis, T. (2020, November 1). Stress and Caregiving. Retrieved February 3, 2024, from Apa.org website: https://www.apa.org/monitor/2020/11/numbers-stress-caregivers*

11 *Nobel, J., Weiss, J., Candice, Courtney, S., & Pickering, L. (2017). Supporting Caregivers in the Workplace: A Practical Guide for Employers. Retrieved from https://nebgh.org/wp-content/up-*

After the sun had set that night, I sat outside on our patio and pondered life, while my exhausted husband slept. One of the things my husband and I have always recognized and discussed in our corporate jobs is how the leadership just keeps assigning project after project and how good employees, at least those like us from Generation X, "Just Do It." These ambitious yet overwhelmed soldiers just keep the ship afloat no matter what. Work-life balance is a new concept invented by millennials and thank God for them.

We all needed a wake-up call. But most bosses don't really care about their employee's work-life balance, not really. The employee must communicate reasonable limitations regarding their workload to strike a healthy work-life balance, but oftentimes when they are honest, the employee risks being demoted or worse, terminated.

Telling his boss that he was overwhelmed and near the brink was a foreign concept to my hardworking man, as it is to so many others. Before his Brachytherapy at Moffitt and even after, I realized that I had been pouring my energy and grace into my husband, trying to connect with him, to help him, to just communicate, but ultimately there was a block. He would not receive it. It has always been that way to some degree, but now with no testosterone on ADT, it was so much worse.

He didn't seem to have any desire to care for himself, so it made my efforts futile. I tried to express myself in any way I could. "Why can't you accept goodness, and why are you such a martyr? Why don't you love yourself?" I knew he had cancer and was getting treatment to get better. I could rationalize that he was on

---

loads/2017/11/NEBGH-Caregiving_Practical-Guide-FINAL.pdf.

Androgen Deprivation Therapy and had no testosterone, but my *feeling self* couldn't wrap my head around that this was our new reality. How long would this new, horrible normal last? Forever?

I got sucked into the storm, and it seemed like all the bad parts about him would always be there and I didn't like the way this felt. I had been hitting my head against the wall for months with this miserable person. The way I saw it was, what is the point of completely investing yourself into someone for ten years when at the end of the decade that person is diagnosed with cancer? And I was mad. I'm not going to be able to grow old with the one I love because it's clear his body is worn out.

Then I thought, "What will be his next diagnosis? He's falling apart in front of my eyes and I'm going to be alone soon." As much as I loved him and wanted to take care of him, it was impossible. I was grasping at straws, and I felt like I was losing my mind. While Tony was dealing with ADT and Brachytherapy, he was also trying desperately to do all the things I asked him to do because he knew he might lose me.

In my first journal entry/love letter, written on March 27th, I set serious ultimatums because it was time to make positive changes. IF NOT NOW, WHEN, darling? Testosterone regulates libido, bone density, muscle mass, body composition, mood, and cognition. The lack of testosterone was meant to starve the cancer cells, but it left his tank literally empty. Blood tests revealed it was working, as his level of testosterone went from his pretreatment level, three hundred and fifty-five nanograms, to six during ADT, all to keep the cancer from ever coming back.

In the spring of 2023, I felt discouraged with him, and I was mean. I didn't want to be mean to my husband, so I took a few days to drive to Panama City, six hours north to stay with friends and to decompress. That's when I started journaling heavily. I would send Tony links to my journal, so he could understand my point of view. When we talked or texted, we fought, so I wrote it down and sent him deep, philosophical journal entries as love letters. After a few days at my friend Marcia's house, working from there, and not speaking to my husband, I finally called him to move forward, but there was still a block. He still didn't understand my perspective, so I stopped him. "Have you read my journal entry from March 27th?" "Yes, honey," he replied, "I have read it twenty-three times and I still don't understand why you aren't coming home." I said, "READ IT AGAIN," and I hung up the phone.

SHARED JOURNAL ENTRY: MONDAY, MARCH 27, 2023

First of all, I love you. I will always love you and I don't want a divorce. I am not there mentally, but I am dealing with some very heavy mental baggage right now regarding our relationship. I want you and me to finally be on the same page... desperately, but it is going to take work from both of us. Do you want to improve? I am concerned about you and that is what is at the center of this. Do you want to get better because I can help? But, if you can't improve, please stop reading and we will need to go down another path.

I am discouraged and I want us to improve our relationship now and forever. I want us to improve our mental and physical health. I want us to live deeper and better and not just keep doing what we have been doing for the past ten years. Not changing is not even an option for me right now. I have this intense and urgent desire to renegotiate everything. What if this cancer diagnosis and treatment is the wake-up call that we need to come out better on the other side?

You should know that I did not intentionally come to Panama City to stay longer than a couple of days, but somewhere deep inside, I knew I needed more time away. When you saw all the luggage, I was taking I could tell that you were alarmed. I knew you would be. I had packed more clothes than I needed just in case. In case of what, though, I had no idea. In the back of my head, I knew it was going to take some time to sort my thoughts out and for us to find each other again.

I needed a soft place to come and regroup and I was not sure of the depth of what I needed until I had time and peace. I needed to unpack my feelings with my mermaids as I have before when things get real. My friends from Panama City are the women who served as my lifelines when I went through my divorce, and I needed an infusion of their power again. My coming here was about you, but it was also about me needing to take time to breathe. We don't take vacations. We work and sleep and take no time to relax and enjoy life.

It's no wonder that after ten years of this, I am tired. We need to start having deep, frequent, and meaningful conversations to evolve past what we are right now. So, yes, I drove away; not because I didn't love you—but because I do love you—endlessly. I needed to confirm my feelings in the echo chamber of my girlfriends. I haven't been doing that. The pandemic turned all our worlds upside down. We were in lockdown for a year, and everyone had their issues to deal with, so I didn't ask for help from girlfriends for years. Not really.

The truth of the matter is that we all feel this way and it's affecting the way we interact with one another in this country. Since the pandemic, time spent alone has increased, in-person social engagement has decreased and now loneliness is considered an epidemic. The structure, function, and quality of our social connections have fallen apart and it's affecting our mental and physical health. In a recent study by the U.S. Surgeon General's office, they found that lacking social connection is as dangerous to one's health as smoking fifteen cigarettes a day.[12]

I love you and you are a good man, so I just made excuses for you because you were better than my ex. So many things about you were exciting and wonderful, so I looked the other way, and we didn't work on you, and we didn't work on me for a long time. We just became these unfeeling zombies, perpetuating our unhealthy character traits, ignoring the things that were slowly creating a fissure. I told Monica what was going on and she shared a powerful analogy. "There is always a crack in the dam." Well, babe, the crack broke on Sunday night, and I just lost it. All the things that I was trying to play nice about, they just bubbled out of me and I was mean, and for that, my love, I am sorry.

It's our anniversary week. Ten years is a major accomplishment, and I knew that this punctuation mark in our lives was worth noticing. It took deep hard conversations with multiple girlfriends—my mermaids—who know and love me and want the very best for me. Revelation after revelation has been leading me down this path, trying to figure out how to best change what's not working in our relationship and our lives, I am noticing it all now, more than ever, because now that you have cancer. "Let's put a pin in the timeline and evaluate where we are at right now." That isn't something I thought about either until I got here and started unpacking all of this... the clothes and the emotions.

---

12 *Health (OASH), Office of the Assistant Secretary for. New Surgeon General Advisory Raises Alarm about the Devastating Impact of the Epidemic of Loneliness and Isolation in the United States. HHS.gov, 3 May 2023, www.hhs.gov/about/news/2023/05/03/newsurgeongeneral-advisory-raises-alarm-about-devastating-impactepidemicloneliness-isolation-united-states.html.*

My time here has been a path of self-discovery, and multiple epiphanies are happening each hour as if I have been asleep for years and I am only now just realizing that I was asleep. I realize that this is the first time in my life that I have been able to leave my home to clear my head, and to make a stand. I could never leave the boys alone long enough to have someone miss me.

My boys are my world and not upsetting the cart for them was always the most important thing to me. But I have neglected my mental health for the benefit of everyone for too long, and I can't do that anymore. I am creative and ambitious. I am messy and I am eccentric. You used to love these things about me. I must start embracing myself and living my truth, or I am going to explode.

Your inability to take care of yourself is threatening our relationship. The dam just broke when we spoke on the phone on Sunday night, and I did not want to do that because it was mean and hurtful, but I couldn't help myself. You have cancer and what kind of monster would I be to kick a guy when he's down? You're on these testosterone blockers to shrink your cancer, and I know you feel vulnerable and sad. You also don't have energy for me... but you ALWAYS RALLY FOR WORK. That makes me resent you and your company, and it feels terribly unfair that by the time you finish your workday you always fall asleep on the couch.

I can't win. My feelings don't even matter unless you say they do. God babe, you have cancer and what kind of bitch would I be to complain about that? I have been biting my tongue for months about these things, but I can't do it any longer. Here is the thing, do you love yourself enough to want to get better? Because you procrastinate about treatment, you don't take vitamins, or eat vegetables, and you won't work out. That has to change.

Your health and happiness matter to me. Most cancer patients need therapy. It's hard, but it's alright to ask for help from me, your friends, and your family. Your mental health is as important as your physical. Sometimes just venting to a friend, family member, or therapist is enough to get you through. You need everyone's support right now, and you need to have these vulnerable conversations to process what is going on. It's not the time to shut people out. It's time to ask for help because we will all be there to help you.

All of these issues were just blurted out over the phone on Sunday night because I had a few glasses of wine... and because I have been holding them in for so damned long. I realized today that the small child inside me had to have a tantrum to break us, so that I could have the week to process our life. I needed space so I could understand these deep thoughts and feelings without you changing my mind with your supportive phone calls and texts.

You would have made me feel okay about all of this, but nothing is okay right now. It's broken and we can't pretend anymore. I must do this outside of our love bubble because I like our love bubble... but there is no room for either of us in there right now. It's hard for me to take a mental break from work too. Do you realize that I have never called in sick, and I have never taken a mental health day, although everyone at work knows that I need to take them?

I am freaking out about my parents' recent health struggles too. I am having a hard time concentrating on my projects at work because I am so worried about you and about my parents who are all in their mid-seventies and falling apart physically. I am in no position to help them geographically or financially, and it's discouraging. And then, there was that senseless suicide on our block last week. Brad's opting out was just the final straw. I really can't believe that in one moment he decided that his beautiful wife and two little kids would be better off without him. It makes no sense.

So, yes, I needed a break from our reality, and the world I stepped into when I crossed Marcia's threshold was peaceful, fun, and soft. I needed that time and I hope you understand why after reading this journal entry.

It's always been that we must work hard and just get the work done. It's our way. But when you don't take a break, you can't see the truths staring at you in the face, you can't take care of yourself or truly enjoy life. We deserve a complete life, Tony. I know that now and that's why it's so hard to watch you pour all your energy into work. Your energy is at a premium right now, so when you spend it all at work and there is none for me, it hurts. You deserve to be happy. We all do, but I don't think you know that. I want you to do the work with a therapist to learn how to love yourself. Until you do that, nothing will change, and I cannot come home.

These journal entries are raw for a reason. I have learned from these hard times. My feelings about our relationship were my reality on March 27th and these thoughts are the best I could do. I have shared them with you in this way because people's reality during challenges looks very different than when things are stable. Our thought processes change from reactionary to rational over time. It's called growth and it's all a part of the full spectrum of being human.

CHAPTER 8

MY ROMAN WARRIOR... SIGH

You may have heard it said that the secret to a happy marriage is that both people don't fall out of love at the same time, and I now believe this to be true, because there were times in the spring of 2023 that the bond that held us together was one-sided and very thin. I also know that it's true that when you are lucky enough to find your perfect match, you hold one another up, and miraculously they give you the strength and hope that you need. It's intuitive and reciprocal and I am so thankful we can do this for one another. Since we first met, that's how it has been for us.

Tony and I are lucky that we have had ten wonderful years together with only a few serious life challenges. For the most part, our life together, with the boys, has been easy and beautiful. Those memories have sustained us in this awful season of cancer. It seems that every day one of us needs the other one's strength in different ways.

Prostate cancer at fifty can't be right. We have only had ten years of loving each other, and now he is fighting for his life. I rationalized all of this could have been avoided if he had just taken better care of himself and gone to the doctor for annual checkups like I have begged him to do over the years. Why are men so stubborn about going to the doctor?

Everyone should get regular checkups, but my husband should have been screened for all diseases earlier and more often because he doesn't know his genetic makeup, but one's DNA is important to understand when treating diseases. Tony didn't like to go to the doctor, but he knew that he was adopted. He long gave up the search to know his birth parents or the story that led to his birth. The state of Illinois was no help when he first inquired as the adoption was closed. So, he gave up the search, but then DNA testing became a thing people were doing to find out their origin story, whether the birth parents wanted it or not. Technology trumped their privacy and old secrets could be discovered just by collecting a spit swab sample. Since DNA tests have become the norm, skeletons are literally walking out of the closet, and the repercussions have been monumental for discarded children of adoption. To find one's family, to ask those questions, to learn the tragedy fills in the blanks in ways all of us yearn to know about how we came into the world.

My origin story mattered and so did his, so this was a process that we started so that he could smile bigger. Despite all that my husband learned about his conception, birth, and adoption... all the scandal, the best part about this voyage has been meeting a sister, a mom, and an aunt who have been yearning to meet him for fifty years. It has been a beautiful flower opening in front of my eyes as Tony completes his puzzle in a way that he didn't even know he needed to. But I knew he needed it, and I pushed for it.

The way he saw it, he already had a wonderful big family and could not imagine anything better. He thought he had enough family already and there was a limit to the number of people he could love, which was a ridiculous conclusion. I have told him that the love that one gives is limitless and he now believes that too. It's been a big year for him.

He once confided in me that he didn't want to investigate who his birth parents were, and especially who his biological mother was because he was afraid of hurting his wonderful momma's feelings. Tony and his mom are very close. They are a big, happy, tight-knit family from rural Illinois. To me, Tony, his mom, and dad, and his four siblings represent a Norman Rockwell type of family with lots of babies, love, and laughter. After so many Christmases spent with them, even now, I think of them in this way. They are teachers, nurses, and factory workers. They work hard and they support one another, and I love and have always respected them all for that.

Tony moved away from his home in rural Illinois shortly after high school and he has never wanted to move back. Living there just doesn't fit him anymore, and our mutual exoduses from our homelands were something we realized early on that we had in common. We had a few other key things in common too. We were both veterans; the only ones in both of our families who served. We both had a high level of integrity and ambition. His ex-wife summed it up shortly after we moved in together in 2014 when she asked Tony if I knew that I had found a good man. I had assured him then that I understood what she was saying and indeed I knew that I had found a good man.

Although we were similar in fundamental ways, I discovered a lot of ways we were different too. I enjoyed getting to know all those things in the first year of dating. I called him Shrek, like an onion he had a lot of layers and I reveled in peeling them all back. One of our life's walks that was starkly different was the fact that Tony never wanted children. Not being a dad put his life on a trajectory of fun, travel, and freedom, while my life as a mom often lacked those attributes. *What could I learn from him*, I wondered. That excited me right away. When Tony was in the room, you would never be bored. He had too many good stories to tell... too much good mojo collected over the years that it spills out onto everyone in the room. He is the life of the party but in a very classy and respectful way. It's sexy.

Sure, Tony loved his nieces and nephews, but he and his ex-wife decided early on that they would instead spend their hard-earned money on big houses, lavish parties, and traveling instead of having children. They also took the pragmatic view that the world was in its current state and didn't need any more babies. Fundamentally, they were right, the world faces serious challenges, and I respected his opinion on the matter of procreating.

In many ways, Tony's decision not to have children earlier in life was a relief to me. With Tony, there would be no chaos of an ex-wife dictating demands to me about how to raise her children. I had dealt with this before with an ex-boyfriend named Darren in Panama City back in 2011. Darren was a nice enough, handsome enough (unless he smiled because his teeth were so bad) guy who wasn't very ambitious. He was *just* good enough, but Darren had one thing that I needed that made me want to pursue him... when I was in Darren's presence, I felt safe and for a woman like me who had been pushed out of her hometown and lied to by the father of her children for 18 years, "safety," became a very sexy thing. My girlfriends all got it.

Our first date was in Bonefish, and he didn't make a good impression. I was not into him when he showed up at this classy bar for a happy hour wearing his work clothes, cargo shorts, an old grey t-shirt, and busted-up steel-toed brown work boots. It was April but it was already hot during the workday, and he had been working on this day. *Sort of sexy, but eh, couldn't he have left work 30 minutes early and showered and changed before coming to our first date? After all, I had dressed up like a smoke show, lipstick, heels, push-up bra... the works!*

My first impression of him was not good. He was balding, he wasn't clean-shaven, he laughed too loud, and he just didn't have much to talk about that I was interested in. But he was philosophical, hopeful, slightly eloquent, and I sensed he was romantic as well. I saw something in him on that first date over a glass of Sauvignon Blanc in the way he treated our server, named Daniel and intelligently mused about Elton John's lyrics of the famous song by the same name. Darren explained to Daniel that Elton had written the song as a love song to his brother, Daniel who was special to him.

I couldn't put my finger on what it was... or maybe I could, but when Darren called the next day and asked if he could take me to Mexico Beach for a candle-lit picnic dinner on the beach, I bit. That date, the drive out there, getting to know him where he felt the most confident, behind the wheel... ya, that date sealed the deal.

We listened to a variety of genres on his radio and spoke about the artists, the songs, and sometimes what that song reminded each of us about... even if it was about an ex-lover. Nothing was off limits. We could ask each other anything and we would have complete transparency. That's how it always was with Darren. I liked it.

On date number two, or as we would later refer to it as, "the do-over date," about halfway through our picnic basket, the sky began to vibrate, and far-off thunder rolled as lightening shards tingled our spines. Clouds became monsters directly over our heads as the full moon behind us lit all their fangs and daggers. Rolling clouds can't even begin to describe what was happening that night. It wasn't that they were rolling, exactly. It was more as if water vapor formed a huge puffy pillow that was filled with luminescent pastel pool lights shimmering to the surface. While the pillows were shimmering and rolling around, sparkling from the inside, the loud deep drum announced the king, The level of the drum's tonality and ferociousness beckoned an equally powerful royal coronation. Stand erect and WATCH, the KING is coming.

And there he is! The king of lightning! And he is here to IMPRESS! Just LOOK at him you fool. He is beautiful! The long, confident walk of someone so important, announced so loudly, as he moves across the horizon from left to right is a thing of beauty, inspiring AWE. Then as the march slowed far off on the right, spiderwebbed off at the top twinkled, and then the king was just gone.... but fear not fair maiden. Even though your friend has been expelled just as fast, look! It is another drum roll and look for it... another royal procession, just as glorious and fleeting as the last one. Someone else important has been announced by drums. Now stop what you are doing, and let's see who it is, what they are wearing, and how quickly they will proceed across the horizon.

Could this be the queen, or the king's nephew, or niece, or maybe this one was his red-haired and defiant brother down the road, or this one... *we were running out of ways people could be related so we had to start getting creative....* It's his best friend who makes sandwiches at the corner deli. *Hahahahahhaa! We rolled on the blanket. And he kissed me. Damn – lightning here too.* Our nature-loving souls became our conscience, "Not too long down there, guys.... keep your eyes open for the SHOW!"

He got up, not in cargo shorts tonight thank God, but tonight, he was in tight-fitting jeans that showed off his adorable ass. Nice. He walked to the cab of his pick-up and changed the station from easy listening to death metal. It seemed more appropriate for this night... and God it was. The loudness of it all fit together so perfectly. It was the first time that I ever actually enjoyed death metal. Now I got it. I was cooler. Ha!

We listened to it all the way back to my house in Panama City from Mexico Beach, about a 45-minute drive. We took in the lyrics. He sang along and it occurred to me for the first time that death metal was not silly or angry, but powerful and passionate but somewhat intimidating. I found that I only liked this kind of music when I was with Darren. Otherwise, I didn't feel safe listening on my own, as I would risk misinterpreting the song. Darren could process the song for me. The words, the meaning, all of it. Somehow in every way, he could effortlessly keep me safe in all the ways I needed him to.

That night, by the light of the moon, the rain pounded the roof of his truck back to town, but we couldn't hear it. The music was too loud. We held hands, swooned over one another, and smiled. We both had gotten bitten by the love bug that night and it felt so good. We already had talked about it between thunder boomers and royalty crossing in front of us out there on the beach. From the get-go, Darren and I were just not afraid to be silly and be genuine with our feelings about anything, but especially about one another.

He and I were passionately in love for the first several months of our relationship. We traveled to Stone Mountain, Georgia for a long weekend, and we had lots of other picnics on the beach. He and I parented our boys together. Hand in hand we bought camping gear, tons of groceries, bikes, and even a motorcycle. I was mostly proud of him in social settings. He was intelligent and a good conversationalist. A big part of me just didn't care that he may be rough around the edges. He was my man and he made me feel safe. My Roman Warrior. My oozing adoration of him was obvious to anyone we met. He made me feel sexy. It worked.

Our do-over date happened, cosmically, stamped with approval from Mt Olympus on the same night Darren just happened to have scheduled a very nice and romantic gesture. It was ALL meant to be. He and I were meant to be, *at least for a little while.* We would both fearlessly ride bareback on our own wild steeds that would become our relationship. We would hold on for dear life and plow into the desert at night. *Scream!* Whatever comes we are strong enough individually to handle it. Let's ride!

That night on Mexico Beach was the most gorgeous spectacle of nature that either of us had ever witnessed. And we had the honor of witnessing it in the company of another human. It blew our minds and from all the storm's erosion of the beach right under our feet, it also *literally* blew our socks off! Surely THIS was a sign. Darren and I shared our first kiss under his beach canopy, sitting in the sand, knowing what was happening around us was a sign that we belonged together. The universe approved of this relationship. It had endorsed it. Darren and I would be one for the ages; that we were sure of. He and I didn't even have a choice in the matter. The stage was set that night under the night sky.

On Saturday Darren had commitments to his son, as he had sensitively explained, so despite our eagerness to get together again we planned to reunite on Sunday at my place. *Let the incessant cute text message barrage commence... sigh.* I had invited Darren over to the house to hang out at noon and then have lunch. The boys were at their dad's this weekend, as they usually were, so the dogs and I had our four-bedroom, two-bath, 2,200-square-foot house to ourselves.

I am a professional, but I am also a homemaker. Just as my mother and grandmothers before me. I believe that a clean house is a reflection and an extension of the hostess. So, you better believe that on this day, my house was clean and tidy. In fact, I had spent all of Saturday making sure it was so.

At this point, Elijah had been living away at a condo on the beach and then with his girlfriend off Thomas Drive for almost a year, and the boys and I were figuring life out. Most weekends, that meant that I was dating or hanging out with my girlfriends and in the off chance I had nothing planned, I meditated and nurtured myself.

Our brick home was like a little slice of heaven with its cold air conditioning and new hardwood floors. From 2006-2013 our sanctuary was a quiet and picturesque, typical Floridian suburbia scene on a quiet cul-de-sac. The backyard held the jewel of the block; a sparkling clean, *(can't you smell the chlorine?)* large kidney-shaped pool with an eight-foot white vinyl privacy fence, all around. It was party central for the boys and all their friends. You couldn't see it from the front of the house, but everyone knew the pool was back there. Passersby and neighbors must have enjoyed all the music and laughter over the years that would pour out from beyond our fence. I felt like a ringmaster and a club DJ for our house and neighborhood on most days. *I loved raising the boys in that house. It was a gift from the universe. Some good karma dealt out, for sure.*

When Darren pulled up to the house in his silver, extended-bed Ford F-150 with a camper shell, I met him at the door. He had his Oakley wrap-around sunglasses on, a tank top, and trunks. He had a small cooler with seltzers in it for us to share and some fruit from the picnic. *Now isn't this so considerate and sweet,* and a beach bag with towels and a blanket spilling out the top.

I met him at the door, anxious to see him again after that electrifying night at the beach and reaffirming drive home. I was looking forward to this but when he walked toward me, he seemed annoyed... agitated. The Small, Quiet Voice from Deep Inside speaks up: *WTH? Oh, gawd! What could I have possibly done ALREADY to offend him? Shit. It's okay; just play it cool.*

Maybe he isn't mad at you. Maybe it's something else. My anxiety really kicked in then, so I took a deep breath. Oh gosh... we need to talk. It's going to get DEEP very quickly. That's for sure. I can tell. God, this guy is unlike anyone I have ever met. It's like he's a poet.

I had the Robin Thicke radio playing at volume level five on Pandora. The house, the food, my outfit, this radio station... everything was perfect, and we were going to have a fun day together, just getting to know one another. The upbeat love ballads echoed throughout the house as well as outside by the pool, and the sandwiches were made. I met Darren at the door wearing my (smallest) bikini, my curled but tasseled hair was falling down around my shoulders, and of course, because I am not a floozy, I wore a cover-up that just happened to be tight fitting around my waist... oh and three-inch wedge pumps. It looked like the sort of outfit that you could perhaps wear to the mall. It was the perfect outfit for *this* day... whatever may or probably would happen today. *This guy was HOT to me at this point. You get that right? Anyway, I love fashion. I have told you that, haven't I?*

I opened the door when I heard him pull up into our carport. I put one foot on the threshold and my right arm up, along the inside of the door, and I impatiently waited for him to walk up to me. Then I said, in my most Barbara Eden sing-song parody of a voice, "Hello Darling! Welcome to my home!" He took his Oakley's off, and they hung on a gator strap behind him now. No hat today. No need to remove a ball cap, as he had NOT done on our first day at Bonefish. At this moment I realized it. The hat was part of his uniform, and the reason he didn't want to take it off at our date was that wearing it all day in the hot sun had ruined his hair... and that's why he left it on that night... not to be disrespectful, but because he had bad hair. Judgment call. My Small, Quiet Voice piped up: *Awe. God. I can be such a judgmental bitch!*

Anyway, I tell you all this, because here in the light of day, when Darren obviously now had had a chance to shower and it was not night, and the wind was not blowing our ears off our heads, he looked good. Here in the light of the day, he even smelled sexy, and he looked appropriately dressed. His hair was combed, and I gathered that this would be another part of the "do-over."

While walking up to greet me, with bags in both hands, Darren said, "Hey," and gave a quick, fake smile. He gently, but hurriedly, gave me a peck on my cheek, then skirted past me in the doorway. Darren darted down the hall and hung a left to the back of the house by the pool. *Weird, but okay. He was just in a hurry to lighten his load. Makes sense.* He carried his beach bag and the cooler to the back of the house, and he set them both down by the door. Then he did an about-face, grabbed my hand, led me back to the kitchen, and pulled me into his chest. Then he did something that quite literally took the air out of my lungs. Darren put my head in his hands and kissed me hard... with all the passion of a Roman warrior.

I am sort of ashamed to tell you this, but it's now January. I am officially two and a half months late delivering on a deadline. Never in my life have I been more than a day or two past any deadline I have had at work. I cannot believe I have let myself down this long and have not sent this last draft to my editor.... This draft. It's now a new year, for God's sake! The holidays are over, and I wanted this done book done way before the holidays, mostly so I could enjoy the holidays. But nope, My Small, Quiet Voice has been along for the entire wild ride, tapping my shoulder incessantly and telling me to get my ass in gear and finish the damn book!

But I am still learning things... isn't that the way the universe works? And I believe that my editor, in her infinite caretaker way, believes that I actually had more of THIS romance story-telling stuff inside me. There was more juice to the squeeze if you will. She knew it. Craaaaaazzzzy! Throughout this process of editing, she only really ever complimented the sections of the book that included love stories and the descriptions of dates and relationships. But in the last few versions (you remember, don't you?) this book has become a guide for workplace culture reform. I don't think my editor will even read THIS version of the book in which I talk about her tough love and guidance. She has already fulfilled her contract, at least six drafts ago! It's okay... she can read it when it's on the best-sellers list and we can sit and drink wine and laugh about what a pain in the ass I was to her. It's a good story to tell around a table of mutual friends. That will happen. I am sure of it.

The romance parts of You Have Arrived seemed to be the only parts that my editor even liked at all. She had been sort of mean to me a few times. Stern, like my grandmas was with me at my mom and stepdad's wedding. Maybe my holding back the romance stuff was annoying her, but she never told me as much. But it was how she complimented my love stories... that input made me start to think that perhaps other people would also enjoy more of THIS. In earlier drafts, she had sensed it, and now because I have lived all of this, from March 2023 to January 2024, not for 30 days, but for 300 days – ten times more than time than I originally thought I needed—it has all been confirmed. "Yup, this chick is a romantic who knows how to recount and tell a good girl story. And isn't THAT what we ALL want to read for fun anyway? That's what makes a book good. You are enjoying our ride together, aren't you? Queue the Grateful Dead... I just have to... I am sorry, I know it's cliché, but "What a long, strange trip it's been!"

Swirly... helicopter... fireworks. *My GOD, I like this guy. I really, really do!* It was a LONG kiss. It was HOT. It had made both our heads swirl on their axes. When we finally came up for air, Darren whispered, his hands still on my face, "I have missed you for each and every moment we have been apart since Friday night. I couldn't wait to do that." He stepped away from me. My knees buckled and I almost fell over flat onto my kitchen floor. He broke the moment. Then Darren shrugged and said, "Now that that's out of the way, what's for lunch? I'm starving and you owe me a meal. Remember that picnic was on me. Now it's your turn, right?" *He is just trying to be funny, right? That's the thing you never really knew with Darren. Was he a comedic genius or an incredibly politically incorrect hillbilly? Sometimes he was one or both, or neither of these two characters, but Darren always kept things interesting.*

For the first six months or so, sure it was hot, but I had my suspicions when Darren and I first started our relationship, and I knew that he was not my lobster. I knew he had things to teach me, and we both had wounds to heal, but he was not my soul mate. He made me feel safe and that was enough for now. When I was with Darren, he knew that my career had been in journalism but at this moment in time, I was working for an international environmental company selling garbage and recycling services to business owners across Bay County. Darren always encouraged me to get back into writing. He supported that endeavor and in large part that's why this chapter was added to my final draft of the book.

He and I ended badly. I broke his heart and he cut off all ties with me and the boys. There would be no relationship of friendly play dates that our boys could have shared. No, our breakup was more like a Greek tragedy, but isn't that what you would have expected from a Roman warrior and his muse? *You Have Arrived* will serve as my message in the bottle. Telling our love story will somehow help others and entertain you and Darren will appreciate the statement and the way this has all played out. He is a poet too and a small part of my heart will always love him.

During our relationship, Darren and his ex-wife shared equal custody of their five-year-old, Jamie, and because of our passion and logistics, my new boyfriend quickly moved in with me and the boys. That meant that I got the chance to love Jamie's chubby little cheeks every other weekend, and three days a week. Jamie gave the best hugs, and he loved me and the boys. We made his son happy, and I knew that this fact was what Darren most loved about our family of six.

Our boys, all together, made a sweet little gang in the pool, at the waterpark, when we went out for frozen yogurt, at the beach, or just playing games and giggling about the silly things Jamie would say. The dynamic was completely different with the boys when Jamie was around. Everyone was happier and lighter. They both became a part of our family and in the end, Jamie was the best part about being with Darren. I stayed longer than I should have because I loved that child.

I adored that kid, and I was teaching him things, important things like how to brush his teeth with "spicy" toothpaste, how to walk upstairs like a big boy, one foot at a time, and how to say please and thank you. Also, the number of new foods I introduced Jamie to turned him from a picky and pale child to a voracious, confident, and healthy little boy, full of energy and vibrance. Jamie's very best thing was coming to our house because there, he wasn't an only child. No, at Shannon's house, he had three brothers who loved him.

Our family had grown, and the boys were all thriving. We were good for one another. Everyone saw it, including Jamie's mom.

Ironically, she was a social worker and she had been formally educated on the best practices by which to raise a child. Who was I to parent her son… and to do it so well? Needless to say, Jamie's mom wasn't too keen on having another woman raise her son. And that presented many problems. She didn't like me, and I wondered what types of things she was telling Jamie about me. Was she using her son as a pawn? God, I prayed that was not the case. That practice can be so toxic to young children.

CHAPTER 9

CONAN

Loving Darren, caring for Jamie, and taking death stares from his mom when she came into the house to pick Jamie up every day... it was all so messy. I realized that Darren had an anger problem and what seemed like his need to keep me safe, soon turned restrictive and suffocating. Even though I knew that I would be breaking up our family and the boys' sweet little gang, I had to ask him to move out. I had been with him long enough to know that he was not the one. After asking three times, after about a year of living together, I finally got Darren to move out of our house. The boys and I were all so sad about it, and by far, the hardest part was missing that silly little monkey, Jamie.

On our very first date, together on April 1st, 2013, I realized that life with Tony would be simpler because he didn't have children and after the loss of Jamie, I was fine with that. I discovered Tony's Plenty of Fish profile on Easter that year and was shocked to see this dapper gentleman in a tux next to the name "Conan," with a tagline that we would often laugh about. My name was listed as "Shannon Joy" and as an homage to one of my favorite songs at the time by Adam Lambert, my tagline on that site was, "What Do You Want from Me." Conan's tagline was a variable tongue-in-cheek answer to my question was simply, beautifully, romantically, "I'll be Good to You." Oh, and he was.

On our first date, at Bud and Alleys, he introduced himself as Conan but kept referring to himself in the third person as "Uncle Tony." His rough misnomer contrasted his sweet online profile and the guy who now stood in front of me. He was so well-spoken, kind, and even dapper... not a barbarian. Conan, though? It just doesn't fit him.

About an hour into our first night together I got brave enough to broach the subject. So, "Conan, huh? Like the Barbarian?" To which he replied, "Yes. Just like that. At that moment I was confused and truthfully, I was a little afraid of what my kids, my friends, and family would think when I told them the most recent man that I was now dating was called Conan (*fill in the blank here won't you:* the Barbarian).

So, after spending seven hours with a guy called Conan the Barbarian on our first date—and him constantly talking about himself in the third person as "Uncle Tony,"— I decided that this is also who he would be to me too; Tony. It made more sense, and it would to my tribe as well.

I found out that night that the nickname Conan had long ago been earned in blood, sweat, and tears by my dapper gentleman. He had been playing rugby for the University of Florida in the early nineties, while during a match, in retaliation for a cheap shot on one of their best players, Tony picked up one of his opponents and threw him, hip-first, into a fence post. The other team charged the field in defense of their wounded player. They screamed, "You're a barbarian!" Tony's fellow Gators were stunned at what he had done too, but being young jocks, they were prouder of him than they were outraged by his behavior. In response to the other team's observation that he was a barbarian, his teammates began chanting, "Conan, Conan, Conan," and the nickname stuck.

Conan stayed in Gainesville after college and for the next three decades. Soon after his rugby nickname was given to him, he started a business as a club entertainer. Eventually, due to his ability to hustle, make friends, and mix songs masterfully, DJ Conan would rise to the eighty-eighth top club DJ in the world according to DJList.com. Then after more than twelve years of playing in clubs throughout Florida, Conan and his wife decided it was time he got a "grown-up job." He gave up his DJ business for her. *I can't help it...this must be said... THIS is the legend of Conan!*

It must have been the most exciting career and he legitimately had made a name for himself in the magical world of the nineties Florida club scene. It was not an easy feat! *Now, as cancer and androgen deprivation knocks his self-esteem down, I try to remind him what a big deal he used to be, and it cheers him up.*

Conan had built a very successful business by following his bliss, the love of music. How many people can say that they did that? Through DJ Conan's talent, diligence, and ingenuity, he earned so many people's love and admiration. He was in the mix in a big way, especially in Gainesville, home of the Florida Gators.

Then, even after his DJ days were over, everyone he knew in Florida would keep knowing him by the only name they knew he had, "Conan." It's just who he was to all of them. and who he will forever be to many people he works with even today, as the misnomer is still attached to him. But to me and the boys, and his family, he will only ever be called Tony or Anthony... the proud, conservative name his mom gave him when she adopted him as an infant, back in 1972.

That first night, our introductions were certainly interesting, but all in all, getting to know one another while the cool salt air blew across our faces was like a dream. Since he was working on

30A, and quite frankly, I would look for any excuse to go there, Conan and I planned to meet on the upper back deck of Bud and Alley's in Seaside which is about an hour's drive from Panama City. I didn't mind the drive out there. I loved everything about 30A, and it was worth it. If you have yet to experience it, I can tell you that the culture, architecture, and charm of 30A rivals that of Europe. It is all so picturesque and immaculate with lots of little villages along the coastal highway, restaurants, galleries, boutiques, wine bars, and live music. It is where I always feel the best. It is my happy place.

That night, I wore my best Spanx under an orange, sporty, cotton dress I had surprisingly found at Big 5 Sports. I still have that dress and I will likely never throw it away. That dress obviously has a lot of good memories attached to it, but on this night, it just hugged my tan body in all the right places and made me feel confident. So did those same three-inch brown wedges from my third date with Darren. I accessorized simply and wore my lucky silver puffy hoops that my mom had given me five years prior and a string of colorful beads, on loan from my best friend, Monica.

Those beads, in every shade of the rainbow, hung around my neck and bounced off the orange dress over my breasts that were standing at attention in my favorite push-up bra as I strode up the back deck. Admittedly I had been primping a little too much at the house that evening and because of that, I ended up being about an hour late for our date. *People tell me that I am always late. I try hard to be respectful of others' time, but admittedly, I have a time management problem. In my defense – in all late women's defense—it takes a lot of thought and effort to get a woman date-night ready and I don't think that men understand that. We have a lot on our plates, period, and I think that's why good women are often late.*

Anyway, on this night, my tardiness translated into the unfortunate consequence that I would not see the sun set from Bud and Alley's back deck while staring into a new man's eyes. He was disappointed because this had been his original vision for our first date, but things rarely happen as you plan, and more often than not big "*You Have Arrived*" moments turn out better when you just let them roll out in front of you like waves crashing to the shore.

So what? I didn't get to sit with him and drink a glass of wine and comment on its splendor, but I did get to enjoy Dave Matthews on the radio while through my windshield all the colors in the sky morphed and celebrated the night. I felt like God was giving me a hug from the safety of my GMC Acadia that night as my view changed to scarlet and tangerine ribbons that traced through the sky as I sped toward my destination.

I sent Conan an apologetic text when I was on my way. In about ten minutes I would be standing in front of him. *I was nervous and I had butterflies in my stomach.* I arrived and luckily found good parking. I added my Acadia in its comforting shade of Merlot to the sea of other mid-size SUVs parked there that night. It was a place for families, after all, this 30A Florida mecca. As I pulled up, as it always did when I visited Seaside, my eye darted to the quaint little post office that had been part of the set for the movie *The Truman Show* that they filmed in Seaside in 1998, the year Andrew was born.

When my date first spotted me coming up the stairs there was an urgency and sincerity about him that I liked. On the lower deck, we said our hellos and he shook my hand. He had a strong grip, but it was still gentle. Something about that first moment took my breath away, and I remembered thinking to myself, "This guy is going to take me out of the dating game." He was about six feet tall, and he was balding, with a scruffy but trimmed beard like my favorite singer from the eighties, George Michael. Conan also had soft, kind, hazel eyes. He was handsome, but more important than looks, he emanated goodness. That was obvious from the first moment I met him. Others sense it too and that's one of the reasons I love to go out in public with my husband. He is just so damned charismatic and it's fun to watch him interact with others. He knows how to make a good first impression and how to work a room, which I find very sexy. Don't you?

"Hi, you're finally here," he said. "Let me put a glass of wine in your hand. Stay right there. Don't move. I will be right back." Then, he turned to order us two glasses of Sauvignon Blanc and he was lost in the crowd. I was standing on the top of the stairway leaning against a post at this point, so I thought I would just reposition myself about twenty feet to the right of the staircase and traverse to the middle of the crowded deck and try to catch a glimpse of the last rays of the sun setting over the Gulf of Mexico.

It was a night full of anticipation and hope. Everyone there was happy, and light and the sky radiated with muted tones now of blue and orange. I was soaking in the atmosphere and getting lost in all the joy when I felt a soft tap on my shoulder. "Hey, I thought I lost you. That maybe you took one look at me and decided to turn tail and run." I assured him that was not the case, and that I had just wanted to watch the last moments of the sunset and get out of the traffic of the staircase.

We laughed about the fact that on our first date, he lost me as soon as he found me. We stood at the top of the world and chatted while we drank our first glass of wine together. As we leaned against the back railing of the deck and talked, I realized how easy it was to be with Tony.

Since that first night together, he has always had this way of making me feel important, treasured, and safe. I instantly trusted him and that was a big deal for me. I had been hurt by the lies from my ex-husband, whom I had divorced two years prior, and most recently by a womanizing Panama City Beach councilman who was fourteen years my senior. It was nice to be with a good man. After one glass of wine at Bud and Alley's, the sun had finished setting and we were up for a change of venue, so he grabbed my hand and escorted me down the wooden stairs. We headed down the sidewalk past Modica Market and the quaint galleries and most of the shops were closed on our way to a sweet old Florida cracker house that had long since been converted into the intimate restaurant, Great Southern. We found a spot on their large patio to sit and order mojitos and conch fritters. Both of us were too giddy to eat much of anything and we didn't even talk about ordering dinner. There were just so many more important things to do.

After about an hour of trying to have an intimate conversation on the bustling patio, a change of venue was upon us. I suggested we sit outside and have another glass of wine at a wine bar up ahead. We walked past the Justin Gaffrey studios, and I told him about the piece I recently had written for 30A.com about the artist.

We got a table at the wine bar and sat with our backs to the street and the white sugar sands of the Emerald Coast overlooked by tourists perpetually perched on the Coleman Beach Pavilion. At the wine bar, we were one of two couples on the patio, and it was pretty quiet. We could finally talk without having to deal with the noise of others interrupting our flow.

Here we could hear the waves and the teenagers who were there with friends and talking about hanging out on the beach past midnight when you were not supposed to be on the beach. We zoned into one another's souls that night and before very long it felt like we were the only two people on the planet. He told me about his life back in Illinois, his two years in the Marines, and his medical discharge the unfortunately ended his military career two years later.

We talked about his ex and why they didn't want children. We talked about my family back in Colorado, my boys, and Elijah. Then he said something I will never forget. "At this stage in my life, I don't want kids, but when I got divorced, I opened myself up to the strong possibility that the next woman I was with would likely have kids and I am okay with that." He enjoyed being around children. That was clear. He was a devoted uncle who never forgot his ten nieces and nephews' birthdays. He had earned celebrity status when he went back home to visit. I ascertained that Tony was the "fun uncle."

This guy was legit. After kissing my fair share of frogs over the past three years, it seemed as if I had finally found a prince. But, I resolved, how would he fit in my life? He lived in Gainesville, and I don't do long-distance relationships, or so I told him. On the first date, he offered up the possibility that he would move to Panama City from Gainesville to me. So, I kept walking down the path with him.

As any single mom will tell you, even on the first date, you must think about how this new man would fit into your already complex life and that of your children. Romance and that glorious spark may happen on a first date and that's important, but a single mom must ascertain logistics, finances, temperament, and so much more for her kids' sake. On our first date I trusted Tony, which was rare, but I also learned that he was intelligent, kind, and ambitious. Unlike so many of the men I had dated as a single mom in Panama City, this ironically chivalrous barbarian was checking all the boxes. To me, integrity was the most attractive attribute and he obviously had it.

Soon the conversation turned to how he thought that children should be raised, and I tuned into his vibe. *My boys' future may depend on it.* He started to speak about his (genuine) moral high ground regarding participation trophies. I listened hard, and in between talking about parenting philosophies, we were eavesdropping and laughing about the loud and privileged teens on the beach who were here for Spring Break, likely from Birmingham,

There was a boisterous and beautiful group of about a dozen kids who we watched desert the boardwalk for the sand where it was much darker. Tony then professed in line with the participation trophy train of thought, "I am writing a book and it's called, *The Wussification of America.*" Well, that was about all I could take. To a woman who was a writer and who was also looking for a good man to help her raise her kids, that proclamation sealed the deal for me. I planted a kiss on him for the ages that would last for minutes. His confident tongue pushed into my mouth and swirled my teeth. His lips powerfully gained dominion over mine as his hands touched my face, the hair on the back of my arm, and my thigh.

That good-natured, passionate, and pure kiss, that I had yearned for because he said the right thing... that sweet first kiss that I had leaned in for, confident my feelings were reciprocal, started our future together. He paid for the tab at the wine bar, and after that, we didn't talk. We just held hands and stepped over the chain that cordoned off the beach. I put my jacket on because it was chilly where the wind pushed coastal breezes onto the Birmingham gang and us. The moon was hiding but the stars were out and on full display. They shined over us for another two hours as he sang to me, and we slid into a new love story and one another's soft embrace that night on the beach at Seaside. The stars, our smiles, our laughter... it was all shining brightly over the deep, dark expanse of the sea.

Flash forward ten years to the day of that first, amazing, and special date. I was now driving home from Fort Lauderdale, with fresh ink on my wrist, and thinking about life. As I drove, I was making mental notes of where I had been and what I really wanted for the rest of my life. Per the podcast that I was listening to, I turned my CRV's radio off and imagined that I was an old woman.

What was I going to say to myself about the life I was living right now? Was I still on course? I was trying to look ahead at a wiser version of myself and then reach back and give my present self the advice that I desperately needed right now. Channeling your own wisdom in this way is powerful. What did I need? I knew then what to do. I heard advice from My Small, Quiet Voice that said to stop waiting to be thinner or richer to start living. It was time to do my own thing and really stop caring about what others thought of me. It was time to just stop letting labels define me. Those lies were holding me back and I needed to just let it go.

Then I called Tony and told him what I had learned. *I seriously cannot believe that I just told my husband that I wanted to change my career path and that I think that my background and expertise make me very qualified to do something new. I told him that I wanted to be a culture coach or a culture consultant or something like that. I told him, "I don't know where this is going to take me, but I need to take the time to figure it out."*

I realized on that day, and spoke to Tony about it too, that perhaps the reason I had not been able to get a better marketing job than the one I already had was because what I had been doing was not what I was supposed to do anymore. I felt that deep in my bones that day and I have felt it every day since. Perhaps my path has now changed, and it is to fundamentally help people. As I spit-balled the idea of becoming a consultant to my husband, I said, "Maybe I'll just fly around the country to different companies and help them." When those words came out of my mouth, they felt sparkly and right. *Thank you, Universe.*

Over the past few years, I had gotten into the habit of signing off my emails with an admittedly passive-aggressive "All the Best" or "Best." I felt like it was somewhat snide, but in truth, I didn't care. I was over it at work so if people assumed that my email ended in a bitchy tone, they were right. What did I care?

But, at this fork-in-the-road point in my life, I had learned some things, and I now I had a new tattoo to prove it. The biggest lesson that had fully embraced on my final day of surfing was that life is too damned short to be miserable all day long. From now on, I planned to put real intention behind my work, and I would make sure that each day I spent would be aligned with this new reality. Now, my new email sign-off would be a more sincere farewell to inspire future communication and would be, "Seriously, All the Best," which was aligned with my brand and my new personal tagline, "If not now, when?"

Over the past thirty days, I had realized that the universe had even more serious lessons to teach me, cancer was in the passenger seat, and he and My Small, Quiet Voice were both influencing my route. No, these lessons were not the type I could ever learn second-hand through a book, a movie, or a sitcom. I had to get behind the wheel myself and go visit my mermaids. Most of all, it was high time that I spent some quality time with myself to discover if I even liked Shannon Joy anymore. It turns out that I did.

One of my heroes, Elizabeth Gilbert, calls these types of hard lessons, "magic lessons," and they are the lessons that must be earned to learn.[13] Magic lessons are the hardest ones to swallow because they are lessons for not only our minds, but also for our souls, and they are always earned out of strife, pain, and challenges. But this is how we humans grow... out of strife. *It really is exhausting, isn't it?*

When I was working at my last corporate job, I was on the road to nowhere, and if life is a highway, I was so far off my route that a severe correction was sorely needed. I know now that I gave everyone around me whiplash when I started this process... and I am sorry for that. But now, thirty days later, I felt that I was back on track, and now, I could really push on the gas.

What I learned on our first date in Seaside was that in comparison to Elijah, Tony was dependable, sincere, and full of integrity, and compared to Darren, Tony was kind, more eloquent, ambitious, and slower to anger. He was so funny, and he also made me feel safe. I had found my lobster but not before being adrift for 36 years, trying to figure out my life and what type of man I wanted and more importantly what type of man I needed at this single-mom-living-in-Panama-City-wild-stage in my life.

Many of the stereotypical challenges that others face when they meet their second spouses were not as pronounced for the two of us, in large part because we spent the first year of our relationship communicating deeply. That's all we had. Our circumstances meant that we lived four hours apart, so all we could do most days was talk on the phone, and because of this, we built

---

13 Gilbert, Elizabeth. "Magic Lessons." Official Website for Best Selling Author Elizabeth Gilbert, www.elizabethgilbert.com/magic-lessons/. Accessed 12 Dec. 2023.

a beautiful foundation of patience, empathy, and transparency. And there was always a weekend together to look forward to.

On these glorious in-between days during that first year when we got to spend time in one another's presence—either in Panama City, in Gainesville, or somewhere in between—we had so much fun and there was so much need for intimate moments of decompression from the stressors of life. We were each other's best friends and one another's alchemists, consistently inspiring one another's growth into the versions of ourselves that would both best serve humanity.

We both felt like we had learned so much from our prior spouses and we were ready to talk about what didn't work with them, and more importantly why. Then we could spin it and improve upon what was now so sweet and right in front of us. We did all that on display for everyone to see, but especially the boys. They were even active participants. The five of us would build a family from broken bits and we built it strong. The boys were seven, ten, and thirteen when we met, and after about a month I knew that I wanted them to meet Tony.

We scheduled a visit for him to meet us at our house for lunch, then we all went out to our favorite cupcake shop together. From there we drove to Panama City Beach to Rocket Lanes to go bowling. That day we laughed at the funny things little kids say that are sometimes wildly inappropriate and not politically correct. The boys mused how there were (oh God) "two of us now," when they saw how Tony and I both liked to belt songs out while we drove in the car.

When he brought up the topic of discipline, on that first day with the boys, I took him aside and explained how I felt about him disciplining them, should the need ever arise. I smiled and looked him square in those kind hazel eyes, and said, "I want my boys to grow up to be a man like you. If you see something wrong, correct it. Keep them safe. Teach them lessons. I trust you. There will never be a time when I will think that your opinion is wrong. I trust you with them, and I will always back you up." And I always have.

Because of this rule of engagement in our relationship, and the blessed fact that the boys were always very well-behaved, discipline was rarely necessary. For the past ten years, the three of them have had the privilege of being raised by an amazing man and they have all learned how to operate in the world using Tony's amazing man code. What a gift Tony has been to all of us.

CHAPTER 10

PC TO GAINESVILLE & BACK AGAIN

FRIDAY, APRIL 7TH, 2023, 4:28 AM

Why does everything that comes out of my mouth when I am home sound like short, disgusted answers? The tone sure, but the word choice and sentence structure of these statements are also completely volatile, and after I say it, each time I hear the words back in my head, I can't even believe I said that. But it's visceral and I am raw, and God, I am really being this BOLD this soon after his diagnosis?

Clearly, I am not just focusing on his prostate cancer, which really is no longer so scary since we went to Moffitt and I have complete confidence in his course of treatment, but I'm like Mike Tyson in the ring right now; unrelentingly brutal. Everything that he has not been able to be for me or refused to do for me since we got together has become suddenly apparent as if all the bad is in the windshield right in front of me now, and it's all I can see.

It's as if my rational mind has been hijacked by my emotional brain because of gross negligence. I love this man and because of it now, I can't think. I can only feel, and I am feeling more deeply and intuitively than I ever have before. It's as if I am thinking with a new organ, perhaps my uterus?

Is this what the wives of all cancer patients go through? If that is the case, there are a lot of hurting women out there. The human condition is shockingly similar. I learned that in therapy years ago and that is why I am convinced that I am just a normal wife with normal wife thoughts, jacked up by this chaos of prostate cancer and ADT. I think that all of this is just part of the larger human experience and now I must be vulnerable and help them. *I am exasperated by all of this already, but I know there is still so much work to do on this book, on my blog, out in the world, interacting with the right people, evolving myself into what I need to be for the world right now... all while being so vulnerable. I am putting so much on the line to try to help others. God, I hope this gamble on me, on the core of who I am, is not for naught.*

Different women deal with cancer in their men in different ways, and that's fine. This is the judgment-free zone. But I must own who I am right now and ride this wave because I know it will toss me out on the other side, but first, there may be some bumps and bruises. There already have been.

Last Friday I woke up at Marcia's and tried to work but I was distracted, so I decided to write the second letter, *Accountability*. Once I started writing it, words and thoughts just poured out of me—like a healing salve—and I found myself distracted most of the morning, knowing that I needed to get something on paper and feeling rushed because our first couple's therapy appointment with my old therapist was at eleven o'clock.

Tony would join us via Zoom, and I just knew that the counselor who had helped me ten years ago could do the same thing again. The day prior I had started aching from my fall that had occurred while attending a work event in Gainesville. When you fall at forty-eight it hurts in odd ways, and I was learning this reality very clearly.

I was experiencing full-body aches and radiating pain down my right leg. I made an appointment at GreenWave Family Wellness Center. The husband-and-wife pair who served the community as a life coach and chiropractor. Since my last sessions with them, they had relocated and grown their practice, but being back in their care was just the same and I needed both of their services on this trip to Panama City.

It was like revisiting all the best parts of Panama City on this trip and I was thoroughly enjoying it, despite the shooting pain radiating down my body. The fall happened at The Fierce Gala in Gainesville, where my company was based. It had been a formal affair that honored the women who were shaping commerce in North Central Florida. Our company was attending to recognize one of our own, Katrina. In 2020 she was diagnosed with breast cancer at only thirty years old. She had to have a radical mastectomy and chemotherapy during the pandemic. And she had survived all that while also overseeing a new construction lease-up as property manager.

You couldn't help but be inspired by Katrina and it was important to me that I attended the event to support her. Since things were heating up at home because of Tony's treatment, this work commitment was the initial push north that got me thinking I could also spend a few days in Panama City to reconnect with old friends and get a break from being the prostate wife, at least for a few days, so I could get my bearings again.

We lived in Bay County from 2005 to 2014 and I had built a good life for us there. Just three months after our relationship started, it came time to move out of the house with the pool. So many of my friends offered to come over and help me pack.

But Tony was the one who went above and beyond with an offer to help us move all our stuff into our new apartment. He even hired a moving company for us. The gesture was so "him."

From July first through the fourth, with Tony's and several loyal friends' help we moved our lives' contents into a two-two with an office at Stanford Point, which was conveniently less than a mile from our old house. These new digs were thankfully still within proximity of all the neighbors and friends that we loved. We would be able to travel the same streets and have access to the same friends, schools, and businesses that were familiar to us, and I would be able to afford the rent myself. This home would be the first one ever that was just mine. Well, at least I would be the only adult on the lease and the idea of that was somewhat liberating.

On moving weekend, a large storm was moving into the area. We busied ourselves with the fun of finding a place for all of our things. Moving into Stanford Point would be the fresh start the boys and I needed. Tony and I would explore our relationship, but I was signing a 12-month lease, and we would make a plan about what that meant to our relationship later on.

On July fourth when we were finally done making the new place feel like home, I was joyfully singing to Bob Marley on the radio, and we were hanging pictures on the wall. I was prepping a modest lunch for all of us, heating up soup and I mused, "There likely won't be any fireworks today. It's a monsoon out there."

That statement motivated Tony to stop what he was doing, unpacking boxes and he walked into my room at the front of the apartment to watch the rain. He noticed that there was some commotion outside. People were moving their cars to the north side of the parking lot. "It looks like your neighbors are having some trouble with the rain," he remarked.

I was spooning soup into our bowls. "What do you mean?" I said and ran to the front of the apartment. I went to the door, opened it, and saw a puddle approaching. But it wasn't a puddle exactly. It looked more like a two-inch wall of water moving with intention down the front corridor toward our threshold. I shut the door hard and shoved the welcome mat under the jam.

Within seconds the rug was soaked, and more water was still pouring in from under the door. I ran to my bathroom and grabbed a few beach towels and added them on top of the saturated rug. Soon, they too were soaked, and water was now coming through the sides of our unit. I thought this was strange because our apartment was in the center of the complex. Did that mean the apartments to our left and right were also filling with water?

Our minds simply could not comprehend what was happening, but we knew this wasn't good. I went into mother bear mode to protect my cubs at all costs. "Tony, my grandma's sewing machine!" The oak cabinet that contained the 100-year-old machine that made all my grandma's baby clothes was my most prized possession. It was also one of the few possessions they moved with when they migrated from the Kansas Dust Bowl to Colorado in 1949. Tony and I had only been together for a few months, but he knew how precious the sewing machine, and my grandma's memory were to me.

Without a second thought, he bear-hugged the large oak cabinet and hoisted it on the dining room table. It was the largest and highest surface we had. It would have to do. *"Pray," I thought, and I did, but fast.* I yelled to the boys to pack their backpacks with some clothes and their toothbrushes and put whatever was precious to them on the top bunk bed. "You have two minutes and then we have to get out of here!"

I moved all my cherished high heels off the floor of my closet and crammed them onto the higher shelves in an effort to save them. The water was coming in so fast, and we were frantically trying to save what we could. "Oh my God, Babe! All the family photos are still in boxes in the garage!" We scrambled to get all the boxes of irreplaceable framed family photos up onto other surfaces in the garage, and we just hoped that it would all be enough.

Within five minutes, the water was up to our knees, and I started worrying about the electricity that was still coursing through the outlets. That was it. We had to get out. We shoved our little dog and big cat into kennels and put our overnight bags on our backs and held all our precious parcels as high as we could as we waded out into the parking lot through waist-deep water. At that moment it occurred to me that we were evacuating an actual disaster. We were doing the same thing I had seen on the news when Hurricane Katrina forced people to evacuate their homes, and the realization of the similarities was surreal.

Thankfully, as I was helping the boys pack, Tony had followed our neighbors' lead and he had moved both our vehicles out of the parking lot, or they would have been flooded too. As luck would have it, I had recently been given a key to my friend Monica's second-story apartment and she was out of town for the weekend, so we headed there for sanctuary. On the way to her apartment, which was about two miles away, we marveled at the force of this non-hurricane. Water was everywhere and cars and trucks were floating down rivers that had been little more than ditches before. The power of the water seemed to have overtaken Panama City in less than a half hour.

While I was inside Monica's apartment trying to get the boys and pets settled, Tony sat in the stairwell and called his mom. When I walked up to him, he was weeping. "Why does God hate me? We did it all right and we almost had you moved into your new house. What the actual f@#$, babe?"

You will hear me often-times refer to Tony as "Amazing Man," and I would be remiss if I didn't tell you now where the nickname originated. So here you go.

The day after the flood, we made our way back to our apartment. Everything seemed ruined, but he figured out what we needed to do to salvage what we could. Tony worked with neighbors and friends and the Baptists who showed up to volunteer, for three exhausting days, he would sweat through his clothes and give everything that he had for us.

On the second day, Ethan, my youngest who was seven at the time tromped through the soggy apartment and stopped when he saw Tony wiping sweat from his brow. My son was genuinely impressed to see someone work this hard for his family and said with his hands on his hips, "Tony, you are the man. Tony, you are amazing. Tony... you are "Amazing Man!" And that he is, and he always has been for me and the boys.

A couple weeks after the flood, the boys and I were fortunate to find a rundown, but spacious, three-bedroom house, not far from either house we had recently evacuated. This new house we would spend the next year in had a finished garage that Ryan and Ethan dubbed their man cave. It was a sweet house close to friends and their school.

My divorce and all the chaos of dating as single mom was now in the rear-view mirror, thankfully. Tony and I were solid and in so in love. We would spend hours on the phone each night for another nine months. As if saving us from the flood wasn't enough to show me and the boys how good of a man Tony truly was, the way he treated me and the boys over the next year certainly was. He was a catch. I focused on this new relationship, and I was so grateful to know that I had finally met the love of my life.

My focus on building a life with Tony meant that I no longer needed the deep and caring female bonds that had sustained me over the past three years. Things were shifting in my social network. I was naturally drifting away from some people and being pulled in other directions now. I focused less on my married or single friends and zeroed in on those who were in-between, like me. My friends who were younger and not married but in serious relationships seemed to offer me better advice, so I leaned into their energy.

At least once a month I would drive to 30A to meet up with Women Connecting Women, a tight group of thirty-somethings who identified as feminists. We would meet for dinner, yoga, poetry readings, or philosophical guided conversations about what it meant to be a woman and the responsibilities that came with being ethically grounded. My friend Erica, whom I had met on assignment while working for the newspaper, had set up the meetings to get like-minded women together and I appreciated the deliberate intention of her effort.

In March of 2014, while chaperoning a field trip with Ethan's first-grade class to Tallahassee, I met a mom who would become a huge part of our lives (and my best mermaid,) Marcia Napier. Her oldest son, Danny, and my youngest, Ethan, were becoming friends and soon after I learned this, I told Ethan that he could have a friend sleep over if it was Danny. I had ulterior motives in planning the sleepover because after our first day together as first-grade chaperones I just knew that Marcia would make good friend material... and her laugh was infectious. I wanted to hear it much more often.

The next Friday after work, Marcia and her two boys knocked on my door and I answered her, "Come on in. It's been a hell of a week! I'm mixing up a pitcher of Cosmopolitans. You want one?" From that day on Marcia and I were confidants and one another's cheerleaders through the stickiness of separations, divorce, new relationships, and raising five strong and confident sons.

Soon after we became really close, which didn't take long, Marcia confided in me that she was miserable in her marriage and that she wanted out. She was considering leaving her son's dad, who was in her opinion, unfeeling and detached. Soon after, she connected with an ex-boyfriend from her college years, then later that year Marcia and her two boys moved in with Mark, who lived with his three girls in a house on Santa Rosa Beach near 30A.

Marcia's new man was exciting and energized, and he became the life of every party over the years that would follow, Tony and Mark formed a solid bond that paralleled my friendship and Marcia. She and I laughed about it and dubbed their special bond a "bromance." Mark and Marcia became our best couple friends and even after we moved to Gainesville and later to Clearwater, we saw them several times each year.

I liked living in Panama City after the divorce. After all, I had a good job as a lifestyle magazine editor, which gave me access to ask questions about interesting aspects of the community. I got to interview and befriend mayors, artists, entrepreneurs, scientists, realtors, and anyone else who was doing good things in any one of the seven communities where Hibu published their Life Magazines.

With Tony, my new friends, my cute little boys, an affordable rental house, and an awesome job, things were good for me and the boys. The boys were also in an excellent charter school, and I was very well connected, which helped since there was no family around. Tony and I started to plan our future together, and he offered to give up his job in Gainesville to move to Panama City.

He applied for a few positions and quickly got an offer as a project manager at Creative Audiovisual on 30A, that idyllic strip of beach where we had first met between Panama City Beach and Destin. I was on cloud nine and loving life, and it was at this time that I noted a stark contrast in our post-divorce scenarios between myself and the boys' dad. Despite ample support from his family, Elijah was couch surfing trying and just trying find his footing after our divorces. He lived in Panama City and then back home in Idaho for a short while with his parents and our dogs. It was such a sorry state of affairs.

It seemed that since our separation in 2010, Elijah was broken. I saw it in his eyes each time I saw him during pick-up and drop-offs on Fridays and Mondays. His drinking and smoking had increased and I started to worry about the boys when they were with their dad's apartment. I didn't know what to do, so I tried to be supportive and often I let him crash on our couch. Our marriage was over, but we were still family. It was an odd arrangement for several months—my dejected but compliant ex-husband living with us and sleeping on the couch—*but* the boys benefited from having their dad around, even if he was brokenhearted.

During the first year of our divorce, Elijah met a wonderful woman named Jinny and they lived together for about a year. She was an anesthesiologist nurse and she proved to provide stability for Elijah and the boys. I sincerely appreciated her as a co-parent and supporter of my ex.

But alcoholics can't do relationships and soon he messed that up. I was so disappointed although I didn't know any of the details. It would seem that the woman Elijah had originally met in a bar and had been dating when we were first separated reentered his sphere... and she wanted him. My boys informed me of all of this so I don't really know exactly how it all went down.

Thankfully, at least at first, there seemed to be some level of adulting going on by someone when the boys visited their dad; as if the adults in the equation were at least trying to shield the boys—who were only five, eight, and eleven—from the chaos of new love and drama. But as time went on, I hated not knowing what was happening when the boys were not with me.

I posted a photo of an angered mother grizzly bear on my Facebook page and a long diatribe about how I would walk through fire for my boys. They were and will always be the center of my world and if anyone endangered my cubs, then they would have to deal with me. I was very protective of them at this time and whenever possible, I would find an excuse about why the boys could not go to their dad's. I didn't know what was up, exactly, but my Spidey senses were going off big time. *I became a mother bear.*

Irena easily convinced Elijah (with the broken heart, now x 2) that if they were living together, he must do the decent thing and marry her... so he did. I couldn't believe it. This union locked him into chaos and uncertainty, while in the same measure, hope and happiness defined me and Tony's life. It was a strange contrast and I remember wishing—at least for the boys' sake—that the drama would soon subside, and things would improve for Elijah. But chaos and alcoholism would follow him for many more years to come.

It broke my heart that he stopped calling or visiting the boys because his new wife was proving to be so mentally unstable. Irena's reactions to normal stimuli were just so off-kilter and, from what Elijah told me, she was violent and self-destructive when she faced any type of challenge. She became ridiculously jealous of Elijah's time spent at work and at the height of their dysfunction, at the pinnacle of her drama, she told Elijah that she wanted to get full custody of my boys. She claimed that because she and Elijah were married, she would be a better mother to them. *My claws and fangs started to come out.*

Irena even went so far as to report me as an unfit mother to the Department of Child and Families. Deputies showed up at my door to inspect my home. They poked around the boys' bedroom where they were playing video games, as well as the contents of my refrigerator. The deputy quickly realized the child endangerment claim was baseless and told me this was not the first time Irena had used local government agencies to do her bidding.

I was so angry at her and for Elijah for inviting this insanity into our lives. If I was nothing else, I was a good mom and I was mortified that I had been forced to defend myself in that regard. Elijah was apologetic at the unfounded accusations and finally told me it was just safer if the boys didn't visit him at his and Irena's house which was located outside of Panama City, in the woods neighboring the bayou.

I was so mad, and I was fine with that request, but I knew that no matter what, the boys would miss their dad. Elijah had chosen to be with a crazy person over being a father to our three beautiful boys and I knew he was being manipulated big time. Meanwhile, Tony and I just did the best we could do to provide stability and support for the boys in his absence. Over the next several years, I tried to broker a relationship between the boys and their dad who was so morally torn and lost. That is something that presented challenges for me, but looking back I am glad that I made the effort on behalf of my sons.

After about a year of Irena creating chaos in our lives in Florida, she and Elijah moved to her family's property in Tennessee for a fresh start. I was hopeful that things would be better for him there, but they only got worse. I would get alarming and sometimes ambiguous texts and calls from Elijah at all hours of the day and night about her irrational behavior, and I was getting more and more concerned for his mortal safety. I soon realized I was Elijah's only tie to the outside world since he had burned every bridge with friends. He was so embarrassed about what he had let his life become. He was isolated and he wasn't going to ask for help. I begged him to speak to his parents, but he refused. He had burned every bridge he had once had as a professional, a friend, and as a church-going Baptist. He had no one... well, except her.

But we spoke. We were still co-parents and he still loved his boys. When we talked, before the boys would speak to their dad, he confided in me that he worried that Irena might kill him in his sleep. What was I supposed to do? He was a complete loser at this point, but he was still the father of my boys and had been my husband for sixteen years. If Irena were to actually murder him, I couldn't live with the knowledge that I might have been able to save him, somehow.

Elijah had screwed up a lot in his life and had been forced to ask his parents to bail him out of trouble more times than I could count. He was too proud to ask for help, but I knew he needed it now, more than ever before. Around this same time, I was working an in-between job at a small local insurance agency. My gig with Hibu had ended, and I was no longer the lifestyle magazine editor that I identified with so well. After more than two years of relishing my dream job, I was now doing freelance and scrambling to pay rent.

That's when our realtor and friend, Stanley Jackson, called and said his friend, Thomas Laughlin, would pay me eleven dollars an hour to help him with his website and to do customer service as an insurance agent in training. I had been a licensed agent at a call center when we lived in Washington, so I knew what was involved, and since he was Stanley's friend, I agreed to it.

His pal, Thomas, had just taken over an established book of business and had moved into what had been Lincoln Insurance. It didn't matter what the agency was called. It was still the office where locals knew that they could get their SR-22 after they got a DUI. It was that type of office. We took anyone. Thomas erected a large new sign in front of the office on Harrison Avenue that read "LAUGHLIN Insurance" and absorbed his predecessor's employees and their book of business. I would sit between Rachel Rodriguez and Jen Smith and be the smiling face that answered walk-ins' questions. It was a huge step down financially, but the job filled my days and once Tony moved in, we could pay our bills.

Soon after I came on board, Jen, Rachel, and I overheard our boss tell one of his cronies that he "didn't have to pay his girls very much because part of their compensation package was living ten minutes from the beach." A hearty, male chauvinistic good ol' boy chuckle followed his remark, and "the girls," and I shared a wide-eyed look of disgust and disbelief. "Okay, so this is what I must do to put food on the table," is what I told myself. It was a lesson in patience and humility.

The consequences of underpaying employees obviously affect those receiving low wages, but employers must realize that undercompensating also limits their organization's growth. According to a study conducted by Flexjobs, 59% of the 2,202 employees surveyed claim low salary is the main factor they quit their job. Consider these repercussions of underpaying employees: high turnover, low morale, poor company culture, bad company reputation, poor performance, low levels of loyalty, and missed opportunities to hire quality talent.[14]

Despite our disenchantment and low wages, Rachel, Jen, and I became a well-oiled machine for our clients. To his credit, Thomas trusted his office manager, Jen, who was a red-headed, feisty, feminist, vegan who didn't fit in with the good ol' boys wives' club. Jen had two boys who were about my sons' ages, and she was married to Ron who was stationed in Panama City with the Coast Guard.

The Smith family tried to make the best out of their time on the Redneck Riviera, but they also recognized that they were too liberal to assimilate. Despite the challenges of working at a local insurance agency, Jen always spoke her mind and was fearless, intelligent, and honest... and everyone knew that her boss respected her. Thomas knew that she was strong and that she would not put up with any of the BS that his clients would dish out. She made his job easy.

I had been at Laughlin Insurance for several months... much longer than I had intended when I discovered I had a few thousand dollars available in my 401K. The stress of not having a vacation over the past several years, worrying about the boys' dad, and missing my family back in Colorado made making a withdrawal seem worth it, so I cashed in the money and told Thomas I would be taking the next week off—without pay of course, because I was an hourly employee—and I organized a

---

14 *Labitoria, C. (2022, June 22). 7 Grave Consequences of Underpaying Employees. Retrieved February 3, 2024, from www.hcamag.com website: https://www.hcamag.com/us/specialization/benefits/7-grave-consequences-of-underpaying-employees/410595*

last-minute, cross-country road trip with the boys to go visit my family in Colorado.

I called it a family reunion and brought Gulf shrimp all the way home on dry ice to make all my cousins a low-country boil. The timing was also right to organize a meeting with my in-laws so the boys could see them and so I could fully articulate, in person, the current state of affairs with Elijah. So, I asked John and Joanne to make the drive from Boise to Craig and they were happy about the opportunity to see their grandsons. After a trip up the hill to my parent's house, I encouraged my in-laws to join the boys and me at the city park to continue our conversation.

We sat under the shade of the cottonwood trees at a picnic table while the boys hit the playground. When they were out of earshot, I turned to them and said, "She is going to kill him. Don't underestimate the insanity of this woman. I know that you don't want to enable him, but the bottom line is this; if you want to save your son's life you need to send him a bus ticket today."

That's what they did, and since then, Elijah has lived with his parents. It's an arrangement that has worked out nicely for him as he was not able to hold down a decent job for many years. As his parents have gotten older, he has been there to help with yard work, shopping, and general support. After struggling with alcoholism for years he is in recovery and has now earned a place there. It's pretty clear that his mom and dad now really appreciate his presence there.

The boys and I returned from Colorado after a week away to find that Tony had lost his job back on 30A. After eight months of working seventy-hour weeks, the owner decided that my Amazing Man was not a good fit. Tony has always been a meticulous and detailed professional, and that is the reputation that he has built his career on, but his new company's pace was too fevered to allow for perfectionism. Tony had been trying to elevate his new company and make it more quality-oriented, but he was fighting a battle that he would not win.

Henry Ford said, "Quality means doing it right when no one is looking," and I loved Tony for living up to that mantra. While delivering quality work may take more time, the benefits personally and collectively as an organization of committing to quality work pay off in exponential dividends.[15]

After six months of being unemployed and living off his savings, looking for another job on the Panhandle and in other cities across the country, Tony couldn't find a better job than what he had in Gainesville before. I was still at Laughlin and disgusted by myself for it. So, we reasoned, despite the boys' excellent school and my deep network of friends, that it was time to move on.

We headed back to Gainesville. Tony would get his old job back, and I found a job as an underwriter at a large insurance company. I was confident that I would be able to plug into Tony's social network and have a nice life in Gainesville. After all, he had been there for the past twenty-five years, and he had an excellent reputation professionally and personally. He was still DJ Conan.

Unfortunately, my hope for a new village was never fully realized there. What neither of us thought about was the fact that most of his couple-friends didn't have kids. That difference made compatibility impossible. Instead of paying for back-to-school clothes and tons of groceries, his childless couple friends all had disposable incomes and we soon drifted away from them.

---

15 *What Is Quality Working? (Importance, How-To, and Tips). Indeed.com, 30 Sept. 2022, ca.indeed.com/ career-advice/career-development/quality-working. Accessed 11 Dec. 2023.*

The lack of social connections in Gainesville took some getting used to, but it just made us stronger as a family. I was able to connect with a couple special moms at school through the boys' soccer games and league ball. I did make a couple good friends, but it would never be like it had been in Panama City when I was part of a village, raising kids, doing life together, for one another. So, in Gainesville the five of us just lived as a tight family unit from 2014-2020. Looking back, they were the sweetest of times.

Then just as the pandemic was starting, Tony found a new opportunity in St. Petersburg, so we sold our house off Tower Road and moved to Clearwater in July of 2020. I kept my Gainesville job as a marketing director. Like everyone else in 2020, I was lonely and lacking connection. We were all hunkered down in different rooms in our house, and even after the schools opened, we had to be careful. No one wanted to contract the virus, but for those who were immunocompromised like Ethan, it was medically necessary for us to minimize exposure to the public as much as possible.

The risk to our youngest son came with a surprise diagnosis of a congenital heart defect that we learned about when he was fifteen in the summer of 2019. I received a call from a camp counselor that Ethan had fainted, so I raced to the camp to pick him up and take him to urgent care to be checked out. The physician ran some tests including an EKG and they discovered an irregular heartbeat.

Despite Ethan's appearance as a healthy and thriving teen, his heart would need to be repaired within the next six months. Surgery was scheduled at UF Shands over Thanksgiving break and our plan was for him to stay home with me to heal until he could rejoin his peers sometime in January.

The company I worked for and is the main case study subject of this book will go unnamed and protected as a professional courtesy. The company is a traditional one that the CEO inherited from her mother, who started the company many years ago and who had since retired.

As president and CEO, Darla wasn't crazy about employees working from home, but she was fine with it for the short term because of Ethan's need for surgery. To ensure I wasn't taking advantage of the situation while I was home with Ethan, my boss instructed me to send her an email each day listing all the tasks I had worked on that day. The length of the reports was always several pages long and she rarely commented on them. I grew to assume that she didn't particularly care about the details of the marketing department since she rarely interfaced with me. I began to wonder if she valued my contributions at all.

While Ethan was still home, healing from his surgery, Tony received a job offer that would require us to eventually relocate to the Tampa area. It was a wonderful opportunity for him to grow his career, so Tony accepted the offer. I scheduled a lunch meeting with my CEO the following week to break the news. I found it strange that my request for lunch to tell her I was moving, and potentially resigning, marked the first time that she and I had ever gone to lunch together. At this point, I had been her marketing director for over three years.

Over pizza and salad, she and I had a cordial conversation about her family and mine. She asked questions about Ethan's recovery, and she seemed to genuinely care about his health, which I appreciated. Toward the end of our meal, I told her about Tony's job offer in St Pete and I asked her, "How do you feel about having a remote marketing director?" She didn't answer but instead changed the subject. Lunch ended and a few days later, on

Christmas morning, Tony proposed with a long love letter and diamond ring, both comically wrapped in Sponge Bob gift wrap

Shortly after the first of the year and before the pandemic started, Darla prepared for me to leave by hiring a new marketing director. When our human resources manager presented me with his resume, I was impressed. The five-page CV detailed his National Guard service, several department chairs, and advanced degrees. This was awkward. I hadn't told my company that I was resigning, just moving, and I was still running the marketing department, a job that I had already proven that I could do from home. Life just went on, and then the pandemic hit, and our plans changed. We took our house off the market, and we all worked from home for about six months. We sold our house in June of 2020 and then we moved to Clearwater the following month. Everyone at work just assumed I would get a new job. Frankly, I did too.

It should be noted that in March, the pandemic forced the corporate office employees home, everyone remained dedicated and productive. The remote work business model—that I had already been successfully doing for two months—was replicated by everyone in the office. As time went on and lockdowns and illness continued, we all stayed home as much as possible to limit exposure. My company tried to keep everyone safe, to their credit, but the work-from-home model made leadership very uncomfortable. They had a corporate office, and they were paying the mortgage and keeping the lights on each month, so they wanted to see it full of staff, although little collaboration occurred there. Everyone at corporate was happier and they even seemed more productive when they were permitted to work from home. I know this because I asked them... but as soon as they could, management demanded that their people get back to the office.

Because very little automation had been implemented our property managers, leasing consultants, maintenance crews, and janitors remained on property, as their work was considered "essential." The nature of leasing apartment dictates that some things just have to be done in person, so supporting the on-site teams' needs and everyone's safety from a marketing standpoint became the marketing department's priority. New procedures and safety precautions meant new ways of communicating with our residents and new signs... so many signs.

Through the pandemic, mostly virtually, my co-director and I would split the portfolio and duties of each property. HR rationalized that I would inevitably resign after I got to the Tampa area, so hiring him would provide the company with continuity. Over his long career, Dave earned a PhD in advertising and had been an instructor of advertising. My new colleague looked excellent on paper, and he should have been a shoo-in to replace me, but what I didn't note from his extensive experience, on the day I told HR to offer him the job, was that all his years in education and as a department chair had kept him in the classroom setting theorizing, but not actually performing the duties of a marketing professional.

That realization came a few weeks after Dave was hired and he started working in the trenches with me. I quickly learned that he had no practical experience and even worse, he had no desire to learn. He was a delegator with no one under him, and that was a problem. Management didn't know, or care to know, what we did in our department, and I was the only one who knew how inept he really was. Quantifying it or even getting my boss's ear to describe it was impossible.

Then there was my constant desire to believe in the good of all people. I really hoped that he could rise to the occasion. I didn't want to bus-toss my colleague to management and risk his ability to feed his kids. Besides, I wasn't a complainer. I was a productive employee who could do anything they asked of me. Surely things would get better, Dave would want to learn, finally pull his weight, and then we would be able to finally split the work up equally... but that never happened.

As co-directors through the pandemic and even after we moved to Clearwater, Dave and I had a daily call each morning to discuss what needed to be accomplished. We would divide and conquer, and Dave would put his duties on his "list." What I soon discovered was that most of his tasks would never make it off his list, however. In staff meetings when Darla or the regional managers would question Dave about his deliverables, his answer would usually be, "It's on my list." Then privately, I would ask him what the challenges were regarding each task, and he would always be vague and change the subject with a laugh.

Then, as things didn't get done, because they were on his list, when our CEO asked why our department was falling behind, I was reluctant to complain. We were co-directors, but I had built the department and all the processes, so if it failed, I rationalized, that was on me. Instead of making excuses for my colleague's ineptitude, I would just take care of his tasks, and his list would magically be wiped clean. It was alright for the first few months, but then he started to take advantage of the dynamics of our department. He really didn't have to do anything, and he was insulated. I felt so taken advantage of.

About a year into this co-director calamity, I learned that HR had originally deemed Dave's contributions more important than mine and his original offer to come to work was ten thousand dollars more than what I was making. Sure, Dave was sitting in his chair at corporate every day. He could attend a Zoom meeting and read the agenda or presentation that I had prepared for him. He could write down their questions and ask me about them after the meeting. He could even send an informative email to the clients regarding what I had told him, but what did he actually do? What qualified him to make more money than me, except his advanced degrees? He had a doctorate in advertising, but what did he know about diagnosing and treating the issues of our company?

Dave resigned after eighteen months, and I stayed on remotely, running the department and traveling to our sites as necessary, for another two years. He found a new opportunity as the marketing director at another large, well-known local company and was provided with a glowing, albeit oblivious recommendation from my CEO. No one was ever the wiser of what really happened, except my HR manager, as I had told her what had been going on many times.

According to the U.S. Department of Labor, women make an average of 83.7% of what men are paid for the same job despite laws prohibiting it.[16] Pay equity is the legal concept that equal work deserves equal pay regardless of an employee's race, gender, ethnicity, age, religion, or other non-job-related factors.[17] Pay equity is important because it helps ensure that all employees are treated fairly by eliminating wage discrimination, which helps promote diversity and inclusion in the workplace.

---

16 *Aragão, C. (2023, March 21). Gender Pay Gap in U.S. Hasn't Changed Much in Two Decades. Retrieved February 3, 2024, from Pew Research Center website: https://www.pewresearch.org/short-reads/2023/03/01/gender-pay-gap-facts*

17 *Nguyen, J., & Bottorff, C. (2023, August 1). What Is Pay Equity and Why Is It Important? – Forbes Advisor. Retrieved February 3, 2024, from www.forbes.com website: https://www.forbes.com/advisor/business/pay-equity/.*

Pay inequities and other unfair practices are frequent in companies with organizational silos, like my last company, where those in charge of setting salaries and approving budgets don't properly communicate with those doing the work for one reason or the other.

Will Kenton, an expert on the economy describes organizational silos as "Business divisions that operate independently and avoid sharing information." Kenton says that a silo mentality can reflect a narrow vision. The employees are so bogged down in their daily chores that they never see the bigger picture or see themselves as having a critical role in that bigger picture, or they may be utterly unaware of the value to others of the information they're sitting on. No matter what the reasons for it are, a silo mentality exists because senior management allows it to exist, and the results are always a toxic workplace culture.[18]

So, on the night of the Fierce Awards, in March of 2023, I found myself back in Gainesville, feeling nostalgic, and looking forward to honoring Katrina, our cancer-surviving rock star. I was also hopeful that the event would give me the opportunity to finally bond with some of my coworkers. I wasn't sure who would be attending but it didn't matter. I was desperate to connect, and I had been working at this company for six years at this point.

I got up early on Thursday and drove the two hours north to Gainesville and worked a full day at the corporate office, then I headed to my hotel to get ready for the gala. I love fashion. It can make you feel better about everything. On this night I chose to wear a magenta velvet wrap dress that highlighted my waist, and a pair of black heels that were comfortable *enough*.

---

18 *Kenton, W. (2019). Understanding Silo Mentality. Retrieved February 3, 2024, from Investopedia website: https://www.investopedia.com/terms/s/silo-mentality.asp*

I was not exactly sure where the gala was being held and my GPS was no help downtown, so I parked in a large parking structure that I was familiar with. Once I started walking, I rationalized that there probably wasn't any parking near the event anyway. My phone's GPS started to work again as I was walking to the venue and I soon discovered that the Fierce Awards were being held more than a half-mile away.

I would need to walk on uneven sidewalks and cobblestone streets to reach my destination in three-inch heels. I felt like a fish out of water. No, I felt like a prostitute looking for her John, but I brushed those thoughts aside and figured that if at thirty years old, Katrina could go through a mastectomy, chemotherapy, and breast reconstruction, all while working a stressful job as an essential employee during COVID-19, then the least I could do to honor her was walk a half-mile in high heeled shoes. These were the Fierce Awards, after all!

The walk to the gala nearly destroyed my ankles that had both been injured years prior during softball when I was only fourteen. That fated summer I would tear the ligaments of each ankle and struggle with twisted ankles for years, until I spent eight years in combat boots. But even after my days wearing a uniform, my ankles were never fully healed and stable, and on this evening, walking in shoes that were way too high, my center of balance was shifted forward and my ankles were not happy.

The truth of the matter was that I was overweight, and my shoes were killing me... but I was fierce. I was running a couple of minutes late, but I finally made it to the event shortly after six. I told my screaming ankles that as soon as we arrived, we would get relief when I sat down. But alas, the courtyard where the Fierce Gala guests were to mingle, take photos, and eat hors d'oeuvres, offered no relief, only cocktail tables to lean against. I was in so much pain, but I was determined to remain fierce. "Okay let's make the best of this situation," I thought. So, I chalked up my mistakes that night to Murphy's Law and enjoyed the free champagne, which somewhat numbed my pain, while I searched the courtyard for familiar faces.

I didn't know anyone there except for the couple who owned the magazine that was sponsoring the event, and they were way too busy mingling with Gainesville's finest to pay me any mind. They didn't even notice me and why should they? Who was I for them to give me a moment of their time on this very special night? I wasn't and had never been part of this community. I was, at best, a vaguely familiar outlier.

I chatted with some other women who seemed like wallflowers too, as I tried to shift my weight from right to left foot to relieve the pressure on my insulted ankles. Finally, after about forty-five minutes of feeling like a loser, in the crowded courtyard, three of my colleagues showed up; Darla, and her two best regional managers, Kelly and Jessica, arrived as a threesome; friends and coworkers and always thick as thieves... at least that is how they appeared to me.

"Hey, you guys, welcome to the gala! Can I get you a drink from the bar?" *They were an hour late and had not let me know that they would be delayed, although they all knew I was going to be here on my own. I don't know why I felt inclined to serve them. I was all in all desperate to be liked and they sensed it.* The truth of the matter is that none of them had ever offered to serve me or make my life easier in any way.

Kelly replied to my offer in her typical sugar-sweet, fake voice, "Oh hi there, that would be great!" I rushed to the front of the line at the drink table, ordered four glasses of wine, and delivered them to my colleagues. It was loud and busy and there was very little inclusive small talk in the courtyard, but soon we were all ushered upstairs, into the indoor venue amidst a new and louder crowd of Gainesville socialites.

Upon entering the historic hall that had recently been converted into an event venue, I bumped into a couple who recognized my last name. They knew my husband Conan and spoke very highly of him. Everyone always did. I had never heard of this couple, but ironically this couple seemed to think of my husband as another family member. So, after chatting with these strangers about how wonderful my husband was, I looked around and my three colleagues were nowhere to be found. Were they avoiding me? It sure felt like it.

I tried to make new friends and chatted with a group of women who seemed nice. I finally found a damned chair, and the nice women sat next to me. We posed for a photo together because the five of us were all wearing dresses in varied shades of pink. *Fancy*. I sat with the pink ladies while we ate our food on our laps and felt like I was in high school all over again. The cool kids, i.e., my colleagues, were in their clique and I was not a part of it. *Whatever, I have lots of friends. People like me.*

That night was an odd push and pull in a lot of ways. There was a group of us left downstairs while most of the crowd had made their way upstairs to watch the awards being presented. It didn't occur to me until later into the evening that most of the party-goers were not amongst us until someone said that there were no more places to sit upstairs anyway so we should just stay put. But I was there to see Katrina get her award. I encouraged my colleagues to follow me upstairs to check out the situation.

We found a place to stand in the back of the very crowded and large room, and we did get the chance to see Katrina get her award, although we couldn't hear the speech she gave. I was able to find a chair for about five minutes while someone else went to the bathroom and their chair was empty. It was disappointing not to hear her inspiring words, but I was able to stand up (and have my chair stolen) and snap a photo of her wiping a tear from her face after accepting her award.

I knew her story. Katrina was my friend, and I was so proud of her, so not hearing her speech or any of the other women's words didn't really matter. To me, just the fact that someone in a position of authority thought it was a good idea to edify women in the community was enough. I was glad to be there, even in the awkward circumstances that led me to this point of the night and the resulting catastrophe that would ultimately define and close my career there.

I thought my ankles were doing better after I finally had the opportunity to sit down, so when we all decided to leave around ten, Kelly actually offered to drive me to my car since it was so far away. *This was a rare act of kindness from her, and one likely mandated by our boss.* She and I and another woman whom Kelly knew all headed to the hall's parking lot together. If we had been better friends I would have held on to her arm for balance, but this woman was not my friend. She had made that very clear to me over the past six years. I tried to move smoothly as we exited but truthfully, I was just focused on walking on my throbbing ankles. I was doing okay until I hit the cobblestone street. My joints were as loose as rubber bands at this point and as soon as I hit the varied surface of the cobblestone, I knew I was in trouble.

The woman that Kelly and I had been chatting with as we exited the gala was a muscular trainer and, of course, being the Pilates Queen of Gainesville, Kelly knew her well. They both seemed very well connected and part of a community they benefited from. As we made our way to the parking lot, they were laughing about something I had no reference to. That's when my ankles simultaneously buckled. I flopped like a limp chicken, screamed, "Shit!" and hit the ground... hard on my right hip and rump, but I caught myself with my hands, miraculously not scraping any part of me. I can only assume that my highly fashionable wrap dress, my push-up bra, and Spanx aided in my graceful descent, but I must have looked absolutely ridiculous.

Kelly and the trainer helped me to my feet and when they did, I took one more step and I was down again. "Take off the damn shoes!" Kelly balked. She was right and I was mortified. I had no business wearing three-inch heels and trying to walk so far, being overweight. Looking back over the past six years, this was the only sensible advice that my colleague had ever given me, and I find myself laughing about it now in irony. Here is the lesson from this very humiliating but life-changing night... *"Don't kill yourself in impractical shoes, Queen. If you are ever out on the town, and your shoes are hurting you, don't risk your safety. Just take off the damn shoes and party on."*

I knew that many of the women who worked at my company were friends. They went to the same trainers and exercise classes, shared the same diet food, and were all very conscious about their appearance, even through the pandemic. They made no bones about sharing their togetherness on social media. I had always felt like an outsider, but tonight, I felt like I was from another planet.

I had been dutifully working from home, supporting the company as their marketing director, and sheltering in place with my immune-compromised son for three years. But unlike all the other women at my company, my existence centered around my family, cooking, keeping a tidy home, and most lately, supporting my husband's mental and physical health following his cancer diagnosis. It was evident to me and to them that we had different priorities, and those differences were clearly on display at the Fierce Award Gala.

But here is the thing, I really didn't care because I had finally come to terms with my body. I love myself no matter what the scale says. I was and am done with waiting to get thin to love myself and put myself out there. That's a fool's game and I was no fool. The next day I attended a big resident appreciation pool party that the property manager and I had been planning at one of our student properties. As marketing director, it was often my job to support the on-site team by taking photos, serving food to the residents, and ensuring everything was going according to plan. I got to the property about an hour before the start of the party and assisted the team in getting the music synced to their speaker and setting out all the food and door prizes.

We were ready to welcome guests, when Jessica, the regional manager who had also attended the previous night's gala, walked onto the pool deck. Jessica had always been kind to me and there was a mutual respect between us. Between taking photos and videos of happy residents eating pizza and playing corn-hole, Jessica and I chatted. She confided that she and Kelly were no longer best friends. She was upset about it, but she saw no clear path to reconciling their friendship.

Jessica also confirmed that our boss and Kelly had indeed been talking about me the night prior. Darla had expressed her opinion of me by telling her regional managers, "Shannon's appearance is really sad, and obviously working from home is not good for her mentally or physically. Look at her with her sore ankles. She is proof that working from home is just not good." I knew there was a high probability that the women had been talking about me, but to have this level of confirmation was rare.

Then, Jessica told me how she felt about all the rottenness of that night and about the company as a whole. Her plan was to just grin and bear it as long as she could until retirement. I told her that I couldn't believe she could put up with it for that long. Jessica shrugged her shoulders and said, "What other choice do I have?" She was alluding to the fact that at this stage in our careers, women don't get to quit. In smaller communities like Gainesville, the business owners all know one another. They make the rules and set the norms and if she upset the apple cart in that community, then she likely would be deemed unworthy of rehire by the others in the community.

When the pool party started winding down, I told everyone goodbye and hugged Jessica. Leaving that property somehow felt very final when I drove away... and almost celebratory. For the next four hours on my drive up to Panama City, I thought about the dynamics of my company and how I fit into it. I realized that I could no longer help these people, as they were blocking what I could give them, and they did not accept me as my authentic self. I never fit their mold anyway, and after tonight I was certain they were done with me.

It was sad, but I concluded that to them, my appearance was more important than my contributions. I had so much to contribute. That was what was so disheartening, but to live my truth—and to just continue to breathe—I simply could not keep working for these people. I was suffocating.

We had been living in the shadow of cancer at my house for four months and I decided that life was too short to be treated so badly at work. But how could I resign without another job? I didn't want to put financial stress on my husband who was going through treatment. I was not sure how, but I had no other choice than to get creative. I had some ideas, but I knew that I had to figure out a clear path for my future, and soon. I wanted more, not less, from my career but I couldn't figure out what that would look like at this juncture.

What I did know, deep inside my heart, however, was that if I could just get to Panama City to talk to my mermaids about my life, they could help me figure out a way forward. For the first time in a long time, I needed them. The waves were drowning me, and all I could do was reach out to my friends for help.

CHAPTER 11

BECOMING

SHARED JOURNAL ENTRY: SATURDAY, APRIL 8TH, 2023, 1:27 AM

What, pray tell, is self-actualization?

One of the most broadly accepted definitions comes from Abraham Maslow, a humanistic psychologist. He described self-actualization as the "process of becoming everything you are capable of becoming." Kim Egel, a San Diego therapist, similarly explains it as the "ability to become the best version of yourself."[19]

You're my sacred mirror! I want to move toward self-actualization too, but you don't seem to get that. I don't want to leave you behind but instead, let's take this journey together. You are a tough and traditional farm boy, and you have certainly never laid your feet on a yoga mat, but you have agreed to go to a ten-hour yoga retreat with me in St Pete tomorrow. That's amazing,

19 Raypole, C. (2020, February 27). Self-Actualization: What It Is and How to Achieve It. Retrieved February 3, 2024, from Healthline website: https://www.healthline.com/health/self-actualization.

and I'm so proud of you. Tomorrow is going to be a fun day. Fill up our cups with goodness.

I confronted you about why you got so upset on Monday when you had to email your team that you had to take care of yourself and take the week off. That was the rawest emotion you have demonstrated since last year when we found out about your diagnosis, and it was because you let your team down at work. I asked you what you thought that meant and you had no answer for me, but I know your heart.

Babe, you live to work, so obviously you are upset when you can't perform like you used to. But you are not a robot. You are exasperated at work, and everyone sees it. You are four months into this disease, and you haven't taken time off yet to rest or recharge your batteries and that is what you and I desperately need right now.

I know you are tired tonight, and you can't seem to listen, but we desperately need to connect right now. I keep encouraging you to push through the lethargy you are experiencing and try to practice active listening to make me feel affirmed and loved and to build trust in our communication. Am I pushing too hard? All I want is to be able to communicate with my husband again. I miss the way we used to complete one another's sentences. ADT has made that impossible now, so we must figure out a new normal.

When I asked you if I could read the email that you sent your team on Monday morning you said yes, but it sparked a conversation about why writing it was so hard for you. You take your professional reputation very seriously. You said that you have been developing your personal brand of always doing right by the client and burning yourself out because of it since your career began. You haven't been on a real vacation in over a decade, and you are burned out and broken down and everyone at work sees it but you. Your fuse is so short honey. They want you to get better physically and mentally too and none of them are going to need further explanation about why you left them hanging.

People are not robots. You said I stole your mojo with this whole process toward self-actualization. Well, hopefully, the mojo we get back tomorrow at Sacred Sessions will be premium grade to boost you to your peak performance.

TUESDAY, APRIL 11TH, 2023, 6:25 PM

You're not in the house right now because you're out teaching Ethan how to drive, which is cool that you're taking the initiative to do that. Now I have only forty minutes of peace to start dinner, get important thoughts on paper, and walk Stella. Ryan is at work, so it's quiet in the house and I'm supposed to be cooking right now, but I must recap what we talked about on the patio tonight regarding health and nutrition because it's important.

I'm reaching a lot of ends to sentences for phrases that we started years ago. I'm making checklists for things and then realizing something needs to be done. I'm realizing that there are some important things that I should have done long ago. I mentioned to you that this process would be frantic and stressful until I reached a point where I no longer feel frantic and stressful anymore and I was unsure when that would be. There are things that I must do and things that you must do and things we need to do as a couple that will allow me to feel comfortable enough to be soft again. Until those things are accomplished, I can't. It's just not in my DNA.

I know you feel insecure about yourself as a man right now because of your hormone levels and I know this is hard for you, especially since I'm not your soft place to land right now. But it is important that I go through this process because I'm not going to stop this process until I get us all on the right track for a healthier lifestyle for both of us.

When my brother shared *The Spark Factor*, by Molly Maloof with me and I got excited about it, he laughed with glee and said, "Shan, you are going to save his life," and that got me really thinking that I could make a difference in your life and in mine by learning these strategies.[20] His words kept me motivated to keep listening and learning, and as you go through the book you will learn too. Let's self-actualize together.

Just know that I love you and like I said tonight, "This is what true love really looks like...it's the best love!" I am on fire and emboldened to learn new things, so we can become better people. Music is so integral to the process. I find myself listening as much as possible. I sing along and breathe it in; Adele, Whitney, Lizzo, Taylor Swift, Harry Styles, Vivaldi, Pavarotti, Lake Street Dive. Those are my go-to spirit guides right now.

I knew last Wednesday I needed to take some time off work this week and I did that. I was on PTO on Monday and spent most of the day helping Ryan process some of his thoughts and I worked a little bit too. I had to since I no longer have any help in my department. It feels so wrong to work when I am taking vacation days but that's the way it is at my company. Maybe we will get funding for a replacement for a new marketing manager, but

20 *Maloof, Dr Molly. The Spark Factor: The Secret to Supercharging Energy, Becoming Resilient, and Feeling Better than Ever. 2023. Amazon, Harper, 31 Jan. 2023, a.co/d/afFVoPb. Accessed 12 Dec. 2023.*

the word from the top right now is that the company can't afford another position in my department.

So far today, I haven't worked at all, thankfully, and I have been able to re-plan our diets, our workouts, and our physical and mental health using what I have learned from listening to *The Spark Factor*. Tomorrow, we will meet with our couple's therapist and talk about all of this. I feel it is necessary to also recap our weekend because the way things rolled out was interesting, and I want to go back and be able to read this later.

We were watching Ted Lasso, which is the cutest show and it's just endearing and helpful and the writers are so eloquent. Season Three, Episode Two made us both laugh hard and cry too, which is rare.[21] The story touched me and made me hungry for adventure. After the episode I was on my phone looking for something to do over the weekend and places to go for upcoming date nights and Sacred Sessions in St Pete popped up.

When I started reading it, it seemed like it had everything that we needed all packaged into an all-day immersive session. So, I signed up for it, and we went on Saturday. I paid for a special goat yoga session for us to attend, which I figured would be the carrot that would get you there, and it was what it took to make my farm-boy feel better about this new, uncomfortable, and irregular environment of yoga and hippies.

As we walked out into the sun after our first yoga class, our bodies, minds, and souls felt stretched and somehow bigger and better, I wondered if you enjoyed the experience. The sun felt good

---

21 *"(I Don't Want to Go to) Chelsea," Ted Lasso, Season 3, Episode 2, Created by Jason Sudeikis, Bill Lawrence, Brendan Hunt, and Joe Kelly. Directed by Tom Marshall, Apple TV+, March 21, 2023.*

on our skin, and I couldn't get a read on your acceptance of this new community of younger, enlightened hippies. I felt right at home though. In many ways, there were my people.

It was uncommonly warm for March, even in Florida. St Petersburg is an eclectic and artistic community and Sacred Sessions, a reoccurring event held at various places depending on the theme of the day, is a perfect example of the type of thing that makes St Pete so special, welcoming, and inclusive. This day was an open invitation to discover new or forgotten lessons. Due to your apprehension, we pondered if we should sit down and speak to Willow, the hippie counselor under the canopy between the incense stand and the people serving up kabobs. We spoke to her and said hello. She said that she didn't have time to see us right now, but she said she would at 2 PM. Maybe we would come back and maybe we wouldn't, depending on the day's other offerings.

We left the outdoor space and took advantage of the breathing classes and interactive art exhibits on display in the old factory that had been converted into a sanctuary for expression and creativity. At two we made our way back outside to see Willow. I could tell you were nervous, and you should have been. This was your first time having your cards read. What did all of this mean and could you learn anything from this experience? At least you had an open mind, and wasn't that the point of this day anyway?

You took it seriously and were surprisingly curious about what we found out from our sessions. My angel number 888 is associated with karma—the principle, in simple terms, meaning what goes around comes back. The karma found through this angel number signals rewards for all your efforts. As a result, seeing 888 can mean great success is ahead, whether it be in career or relationships. It was an informative and reaffirming session that

I should keep discovering who I am and embrace all the good in the universe.

With you though, in every deck she presented, Willow kept finding cards that said you needed to be more empathetic and vulnerable to relate to people with your feminine side. She said that we all have half-feminine and half-masculine energy. She had you pegged as such a guys' guy. She was right when she said that you manage that energy so well, but the other half of your energy is lying dormant. The cards and Willow's intuition was strong about this: if you could tap into your feminine side your career and life would just take off. Willow went on to say that you should meditate with a blue stone to find peace. Your angel message is 333, which encourages you to put plans into action, let your strength be the guide, trust yourself, and put thought into your choices. This angel number also relates to optimism, creativity, and intuition. She summarized that masculine energy is blocking growth.

Everything we learned about you today pointed to feminine energy being blocked and I find that so interesting because I am here for you as a fully feminine source of energy... but you need more. Who is looking for you? *Who are you looking for? Perhaps time will tell and perhaps the DNA test that awaits you back at the house will give us more answers to the questions we are seeking.*

The results of our tarot card readings seemed accurate, and it was just fun to explore the energy of the metaphysical. I don't know how much stock either of us should put into those readings, but we left Willow feeling lighter, brighter, and more optimistic about the future and that was a relief.

I hope that some of the personal growth we need to do will also be provided by the books that we brought home from Sacred

Sessions. Reading is something I have wanted to start doing more of for a long time. We bought twelve used books for twelve dollars. It's a virtually free new library of varied topics that I know will help us in lots of good ways.

I also took a lot of photos of you today, and some of them spoke to me. There was a lot of unique urban art there on display that created interesting conversations. There was one sculpture that had an Andy Warhol quote about men preferring to be a machine, and I took your photo next to the sculpture. It was as if standing by that sculpture and connecting with the image and having your photo taken in front of it was a pivotal moment for you to recognize your challenges, and it was also an invitation to let go and to change. Yesterday was pure magic and I am so glad I took so many photos of us together there.

I just met the sweetest couple on the trail for our afternoon walk around the pond. Of course, Stella had to say hello to them with her cute little bulldog butt shake. The man had a Moffitt Cancer Center fundraiser sweatshirt on, so I said that I liked his shirt and that we recently discovered the cancer center and now knew what that place was all about. They both chuckled, and I asked, "Are either of you a cancer survivor?" and the woman said, "Yes. I am a survivor of breast cancer."

We chit-chatted a bit and talked about her treatment and what Tony's treatment would be like there and at the VA. I told them that after last Wednesday's appointment, at Moffitt we both felt so much better about the treatment plan.

Then, out of nowhere—because I have never thought this or said it out loud before—this wisdom just came out of my mouth in a way that shocked me. I truthfully couldn't even believe that it was me who was saying it, but when I saw the empathy on their faces, I said, "You know, when cancer touches your life, it is so tough and it affects every aspect of your life, in ways that you can't even imagine." That was the first time I realized what was happening in my heart and all around me, and I started to realize that perhaps something good could come out of this cancer journey.

I have heard people talk about this cancer club before on talk shows and it sounded so cliché saying that Tony's diagnosis had in some ways been a gift, but somewhere inside of me, I guess that I needed two strangers to confirm that I was not going crazy. When we spoke to one another, there was a mutual understanding of empathy, and for the first time, I realized that I was part of a club of people I never wanted to be a part of.

WISDOM WOMAN: BY PA KUSHNER

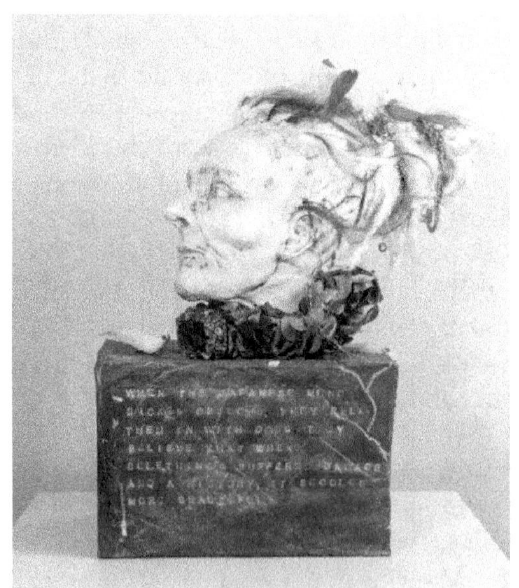

INSCRIPTION: *When the Japanese mend broken objects, they fill them with gold. They believe that when something suffers damage and a history, it becomes more beautiful.*

Known as kintsugi, this ancient practice is also about forgiveness. It's a practice of self-love which is very much in line with the concept of self-actualization. Accepting your cracks means being accepting and loving toward yourself. You must forgive yourself first, before you are capable of forgiving another. The concept of kintsugi was also featured on Ted Lasso on Friday, and it came up in a recent discussion with Monica last week, too.

It would appear that the universe keeps reminding me of the concept of kintsugi and I am listening. Now, here is the icing on the cake for me regarding this school of thought. PA is a neighbor who lives five doors down. I met her on the trail too, or perhaps I should say that Stella met her dog, Polo and PA and I are just along for the ride. As luck would have it, their walks have frequently been occurring at the same time, so Polo and Stella, along with PA and I have been getting to know each other well over the past year.

My strong, funny, and wise neighbor, PA is about ten years older than me. She is the mother of two sons. One of them lives in Colorado and the other lives in heaven. Her spirit and talent have bowled me over. Her beautiful and welcoming home also serves as an exhibition space for dozens of the evocative and sometimes provocative sculptures she has made over the years. Her work took a turn toward grief recovery and inward love when her son passed away. Her art was cathartic for her too, just as mine has been.

PA has also reluctantly become a member of a club she never wanted to be part of, but she also found ways to give back. She formed the I'M LOGAN IT Foundation in her son's memory with the goal of reminding each of us to always give 150% effort in everything we do and to always be there to lend a hand to help those in need.

Understand that her work is all stunning and meaningful. PA's sculptures speak to the eyes, the heart, and the soul, and this specific sculpture is one that I am committed to adding to my home one day. I absolutely love it. The lessons of kintsugi are ones I have completely embraced and the woman's face that my artist friend's hands have brought forth from nothingness in clay reminds me of my own mother's face. To view this piece in person is a celebration of love, life, and community and it is a serious meditation catalyst for me.

PA has many sculptures in her home, but it is this one that most resonates with me because of the message on the plaque and composition and the fact that it is a communal art piece. In fact, each piece of hair sewn into the elaborate updo was donated by her friends. The various shades and textures of hair come together to represent a diverse village of women who love and support one another. It's a piece that her sons and my sons can get behind and it represents the greater community of caring people, globally, from whom we can draw help, strength, and wisdom.

IN LOGAN'S MEMORY, HERE ARE TEN WAYS TO I'M LOGAN IT:

1. Smile and say hello to strangers
2. Be funny and make someone laugh
3. Give someone a hug who looks like they need one

4. Strike up a conversation with someone you don't know
5. Do a "dance of joy" for someone close to you
6. Play sports with people you don't know in the park
7. Connect two friends who had not met previously
8. Spend time with a friend who's feeling down
9. Reach out and help a young kid or an elderly person
10. Send a thank you note to a teacher/coach who inspired you

---

WEDNESDAY, APRIL 12, 2023 – 1:32 PM

In the Walgreens Parking Lot

I think I am having a nervous breakdown. I took precious PTO this week to try to get some things straightened out; my work computer issues, sending an inhaler to Andrew out in Boston, and just random errands that need to get done for my family and myself. It would be nice to use my time off to unwind right now too. Heaven knows I could use some fun time alone or even with the family. All we ever do is work, work, work.

But this is my third day off so far, and I don't feel like I have had any semblance of a vacation. What a waste of those precious days earned. We used to go away on long weekends and spend those precious days recharging, unplugging, and adding to our memory bank with positive light.

However, the last three days off from work have consisted of running errands, work meetings, self-help books, and trying to put my marriage back together. I feel like I am drowning and there is not enough time to get myself saved. I have been earning vacation hours and have accrued 100 hours, but with no one to help me in my department, I can't take time off. I want to get off this hamster wheel and throw my phone out the window, let it shatter on the rain-soaked black top, and just drive away.

Seriously, is this how I spend my days off now? I need a break. Truthfully, I needed a vacation six months ago and I told Tony that six months ago, but something kept coming up, or we couldn't afford it. His constant travel schedule at work meant we couldn't plan anything for us because we never knew when he would be gone from month to month. I was already stressed out and then we got the cancer diagnosis. I just didn't have the bandwidth to deal with this. I knew it then and I certainly know it now.

This is not what vacation is supposed to look like... sitting in the Walgreens parking lot, trying not to have a panic attack. This is maddening and it's happening to so many people. How can we strike a work-life balance if work needs us even on our days off and each evening?

Can one person really make a change that can help this issue? I am sure going to try. Jesus take the wheel!

CHAPTER 12

THE SMALL, QUIET VOICE

MONDAY, APRIL 17, 2023 – 9:23 PM

I'm walking through our neighborhood tonight and trying to figure out why I'm so upset. I am just tied up in knots and cannot be a mom and wife and maid in that house for another minute. I don't know exactly what's wrong. I just know that it's been a really tough day. I need to breathe and try to listen to my spirit, and not my mind. Truthfully, none of them function very well in that house any longer. That scares me. Is it because we work from home? Home isn't a refuge for me anymore. It is just the place where I have to work.

Tony and I have both worked from home, here in Clearwater, more than in any other place we have lived. Home should be a sanctuary. I am learning this the hard way. This domestic diva, whom I dubbed myself when we lived in Panama City when I would make meals for the busier mommas in my Mothers of Preschoolers group, this better-than-average mom of three, this self-proclaimed homemaker may have destroyed the space that was supposed to offer her comfort.

Now, stress paints the walls of this house like a demented Salvatore Dali melting clock. Okay... breathe. I need to unpack this in my head. I feel like I am walking through the house at a forty-five-degree angle... I am crooked, but if I walk far enough, maybe I will straighten back out again. I need a walk.

The only time I have ever felt like this before was when I was thirty-six with three little boys. I was on fire to make a change then too; to discover who I really was. Looking back to the summer and fall of 2010, I was frantic, angry, and crazy then too. The only explanation for it then, and again now, is that it is finally time to listen to the Small, Quiet Voice Inside. I can't ignore it any longer.

It would usually happen when I would drive, and I drove a lot at the time because I was on the praise and worship team at our Baptist church. I didn't just go for an hour on Sunday mornings like the rest of the flock. No, I was a worship leader, and I was serving with two or three other men and women, plus everyone in the choir. All in all, my network was at the church and especially the music department. I love the creatives. The thing about this group of Christians that my liberal, independent mind accepted, was that they were real. They all admitted they had flaws. They were willing to help you in your time of need too. They showed up for one another and I appreciated that.

I performed praise and worship for over three years when we lived in PC. I would read the words on the back wall, and lead the followers in singing the lyrics, hitting the right notes, clapping, and timing, but it was also something more. I felt like when I was on stage, leading praise and worship, and when I was singing in the choir, that I was in the groove with one of my God-given talents. On stage, I was channeling goodness and sending it back to those sitting in the pews. Was it the goodness of my grandmother, or perhaps God? I could never be sure, but I think it was all of that... and more.

It was a time in my life when I was trying to figure myself out. I seem to fit in well with the music department servants because of that. The drive to church took me down a winding road of car dealerships and grocery stores. Twenty-third Street careened around the college and across the Hathaway Bridge, and then it opened to a smooth-flowing stretch on Back Beach Road. I would swing left and cut through an upper-middle-class neighborhood, park my light blue Dodge Grand Caravan in the first space by the back door, and enter the music room. I would slide in the door to be welcomed like Norm from *Cheers*. It was at a time in my life when I only got away from the rigors of being a wife, a mother, and an online student when I went to church on Sundays from seven to noon and on Wednesdays from five to nine. I liked the way I fit in there.

I would do that drive, back and forth, four times each week and it would give me time to think and pray. During that time, I was awoken by that Small, Quiet Voice from deep inside my uterus, throat, and mind and she was telling me that an escape was now possible. Can I really leave Elijah? I think I can. After all, I have earned my degree now. The boys are all in school and Andrew is probably mature enough to watch his brothers after school, so daycare costs won't be an issue. I certainly can't afford daycare but now that I have my degree and a decent job, I should be able to afford to keep the lights on.

During this time, as a young mother, struggling with her anger toward her husband, while trying to be a leader at my church, I was in constant struggle. Then *she* would whisper to me in my dreams, and I would usually ignore her. Then, she would sneak around the next night to my belly to try to make me understand. If my stomach ignored her, she would try my throat. If my throat resisted, she would find her way into my dreams, throw herself against the glass wall of my psyche, and demand attention. Even though the Small, Quiet Voice was in a straitjacket, blindfolded, with a gag, she will not be ignored... because she can still hear, and she knows you aren't doing her bidding. *You see?*

At this time in my life, I desperately wanted to be a good mom and wife and I certainly didn't want to be a statistic. I liked the stability of being married for me and the boys. I had built my life around the reputation that came from being married to a handsome man. We appeared to be happy and functioning, but we weren't. Very few people knew what was happening. My music pastor and his wife, who became dear friends, knew our struggles, but it wasn't until I got counseling from our head pastor that I decided I wanted to file for divorce.

Brother George was a good man and I trusted him. He had been through a divorce too. He also had degrees in pastoral studies and counseling, and I knew that he legitimately cared about me and my young family. I didn't want to blow up my life and I didn't want to be a statistic. I had been so stubborn for so long; I had been trying to fix a man who could not be fixed. Brother George gave me the Godly, father-figure permission that he was uniquely qualified (at least in my mind at the time) to give so that I could break free. He granted me permission to get a divorce and he did one more in a stern, caring way, he told me that God didn't want me to be miserable, living with a liar for the rest of my life. He asked me why I thought I needed to stay and block God from sending me my real husband... as this one was an imposter.

After I left that counseling session, I had a dilemma; if I filed for a divorce, I could no longer lead praise and worship. Could I even attend services anymore? I would be off-brand for any church during this stage of my life. Things were about to change in innumerable ways for me.

Here's what I have learned. You must listen to your gut, your conscience, your SQV, God, the Universe, whatever you want to call it. I believe that my Small, Quiet Voice is the protector of my very soul, and from deep inside... she walks hand in hand with my conscience. They make deals all the time. Conscience says things like, "I know I shouldn't have another child with this man," but she negotiates... "We do have more love to give, after all. Your momma had four children and if she could do four, you can do three. Besides, you can probably get your college degree by the time the baby has to go to school." *She* is a VERY good negotiator.

She and Conscience are at war all the time. If you can hear her, walk tall, but if your Small, Quiet Voice has not been listened to, and is silent, she is likely scared or ashamed and can't help you. She just sits in the corner of that square glass room and rocks back and forth. She is bound and gagged, far away from your waking thoughts because Conscience is quite frankly, embarrassed about what he has done. He has silenced and ignored her for so long and she must fight like hell to be noticed. But when you finally do hear her, always listen.

In 2010, I had to listen to her, or I thought I would die. Now just as it was then, during my divorce with Elijah it's as if I'm excavating my former self with the frantic urgency and passion of a woman who has been bound and gagged, oppressed, and pushed down. I don't know what I want now. Do I want a divorce again or do I just need to rearrange some things in my life? I feel like after twenty-five years of being a mom and working that I just need to press the pause button to find out what I need.

I used to love cooking meals, cleaning the house, and taking good care of my family. Now, I'm just tired of doing it all and nagging them all the time to help me, and I don't want to do any of it anymore. Ethan is graduating soon, and I sense a new stage in our lives now that the school system is no longer a consideration. Ryan and Ethan may be moving out very soon, and I wonder what will life look like for Tony and me then... without the structure that being co-parents has meant to us since we first started this relationship ten years ago.

I rationalize that many mothers must feel this way when they are contemplating their empty nest. Still other parents feel a part of their heart has left when their kids leave the nest. I have had enough therapy to know that there is no right way to internally process big-life events. Your way is the right way. But I laugh now at the reality of my current mental state and how wrong society says I am to have these thoughts because the only sentiment I can ever remember any mom of young adults expressing was that they were, "sad those days were over." Yes, indeed. My feelings about our children's departure is quite different from those of my friends on Facebook, but I am not going to make any apologies for it.

I am exhausted mentally, physically, and spiritually, and my husband who has sacrificed everything to help me raise these kids was just diagnosed with cancer. We have been putting off our honeymoon for two years and we haven't had a proper vacation since we met because we have been spending all our time and money on the kids.

Now, he is required to take medicine to make him less of a man to treat a deadly disease, so my life's current dichotomy is to let modern medicine literally knock my husband to the ground when he deserves to be lifted up the most, or do nothing and let him die? That's not fair! *In that moment I heard my mother's voice: No one ever said life would be fair, darling. In fact, life is more like a bowl of cherries, full of pits.*

When you contemplate my perspective, it really does boggle the mind. Over the past ten years, Tony and I have rarely had a moment or weekend alone because Elijah didn't help, he lived eight states away and he never took them. So much energy was diverted to make sure the boys were okay... and for the most part, they are.

Financially, the drain of raising three kids is astronomical and I refuse to try to quantify the investment as I know it will send me into a deep depression. Let's just say that we paid for everything, so every dime we ever earned was spent on raising them. For most of those years, we didn't receive child support and I felt guilty about it because these weren't even Tony's kids.

To keep the lights on, the way our finances always worked was that Tony would have to pay at least an extra $800 more than me each month. These were my kids, but I couldn't afford to raise them without my ex-husband's help. It was so embarrassing. Then again, Elijah couldn't hold down a job and that was not my fault. So instead, I was lucky enough to find an amazing and generous man who didn't make me feel bad about how much he had to help financially. However, this indebtedness to my spouse made me feel sorry, less than, as if I had to be nicer than I wanted to be sometimes, and more compliant than I should have to be. It put a negative imbalance of guilt on our love, and we needed to sort it out, now that the boys were (mostly) gone.

Despite the time, energy, and financial challenges, Tony and I were committed to giving OUR boys every advantage we could. We were showing up for them, no matter what, as their parental unit. So, because their dad couldn't function as a responsible adult, every holiday we had the boys. Elijah never called, even on their birthdays.

During the global pandemic and shelter in place, it was the five of us against the world. Throughout their childhoods Tony and I were the ones examining every grade, worrying about their emotions, making sure they flossed, ensuring they got enough calories and vitamins, and that they all had healthy social lives. It was us driving Andrew to Georgia to run in a one-hundred-mile trail race twice in two years. It was us making sure they had the right shoes for the sport they were in, or to give them a boost of confidence in the halls. Tony and I made sure that the boys had cool clothes like their friends, the right prescription glasses, and cars that were safe and dependable.

This is important too… because their dad had a disease, Tony, in his perpetually classy way, never bad-mouthed him because he knew that would only hurt the boys and his relationship. Tony and I would be all of it for them, so we got to be the ones to encourage the boys to go out for extracurricular activities and clubs that fit their personality, never mind if getting them there was a complete inconvenience. Tony and I would be the ones fighting the schools, so they didn't have to be vaccinated, attending the PTO meetings, fundraising, and advocating for them when they struggled in school or were mistreated by a teacher or a classmate. We would be the ones to get that call at work and speed across town when one of them would get into a car accident.

Tony and I were the ones coordinating medical care for our son, who we discovered had an undiagnosed congenital heart defect. We also got to be the ones to see Ethan's body heal and his confidence skyrocket through that major health scare.

No one else but he and I were there… surviving and rebuilding after the flood, double-checking every day that they had inhalers in their backpacks and encouraging them to get their first jobs. And here's the thing, he didn't have to do any of it. Even though he could have told me no thank you, "I don't want to be the father of three kids who are not mine," like so many other guys told me when I was dating in Panama City, Tony showed up for us every day and in every way. Now I just wanted to shower my husband with the love and appreciation that he had earned. I wanted to be able to look into his eyes and connect with him in deeper and more significant ways. That is what he deserved... but cancer, seriously? Cancer, NOW?

Being a parent is wonderful, but it's also a hundred things each day you must do, or someone could die. It's not for the weak of heart, but together, alone, out here in Florida, we made it look easy. And I know, life isn't easy nor is it fair, but at this point, we thought we had added enough good stuff to our karma cups to finally get a break. I had been a good mom and Tony had been the best "mom's boyfriend" and stepdad for the past ten years—even though he never even wanted kids—and now we desperately wanted to travel like other couples. We wanted some alone time and to enjoy one another's company without CONSTANTLY PARENTING. Ya, empty nest syndrome... it's a thing.

But we won't be empty nesters anytime soon. We still have one that has failed to leave the nest. While our oldest is independent and has graduated from college, struggling in Boston, but building his life nonetheless, and our youngest is now living with his dad and grandparents, figuring out what he wants from life, our middle son, Ryan is struggling.

He graduated in 2019, then his brother had open heart surgery, then the world got a virus, and political and racial tensions exploded. Keep it all in context for his generation... the world has not been a happy place to launch into. Since Ryan graduated high school, our boy who is highly empathetic has had to work in retail with a mask on, and take classes online to earn his degree, all while just pretending that everything is okay in the world, but it's not.

Because we moved in the summer of 2020 during the pandemic, in forced isolation, Ryan has struggled to make new friends in this new town. To replace those important connections over the years, his social media consumption has become nearly constant. He finds many of his friends in the video games he plays and lacks the traditional friendships and connections that I want for him.

Since Ryan graduated, our world has been plagued by social and political unrest all throughout the world. Protests and demonstrations are being held in response to issues of police brutality, racial inequality, and political corruption. The U.S also held presidential elections in 2020, which were marked by the near collapse of our democracy. Social media just fuels all the hate and divisive rhetoric.

Let's not forget that we live in Florida, a place where the effects of global warming are very apparent with rising sea levels, record-high temperatures each summer, and frequent hurricanes. Living in Florida provides a constant reminder that the environment is changing. Across the globe natural disasters have greatly increased from heatwaves in Europe, tsunamis in southwest Asia, draughts in Africa, volcanic eruptions, melting polar ice caps, U.S, wildfires, hurricanes, and earthquakes. It's a scary time to launch.

All of this is what we are asking our son to "launch" into. He is embarrassed to be white, and ashamed of all three of his parents who served in the military. He is outraged by the war in Palestine, and his anxiety about it is often too high for him to enjoy a meal. To escape the darkness, depression, and reality of his life, because he hasn't made friends in this new town, he plays video games with others online. That's his life.

To be completely transparent, the above is my interpretation of my son's current mindset, but he is his own person. He is a passionate civil rights activist in his own right and at 22 years old he has discovered his own principles. We align on most of these things, but his media consumption far surpasses my own, that is why, in month ten of this process I asked my son, Ryan (which is not his real name) to read what I had written about him.

After some healthy debate, I decided that I would give him the liberty to write his own opinion of his current station in life. I share it with you now because I believe many young people believe the same things. Ryan and I and Tony have been talking about these issues and his opinions for years and we try (but usually fail) to give him the feedback that he deserves. A revolution is coming and as leaders, we need to not turn a blind eye to this generation's concerns but instead, empower them to continue to research, explore, and form their own value opinions. I am so proud of my son.

EMAIL FROM RYAN, JANUARY 22ND, 2024

I am not embarrassed to be white, but I do recognize the system of white supremacy when it is glaring at me in the face. It makes me angry when white neoliberals pretend to be friends with black people while using individualism as a cop-out for not benefiting from white supremacy. Here's what many good white people say when the topic of white privilege is brought up; "You think I'm privileged? I have never gotten a dime I didn't have to earn. I had to build my life from nothing too."

As someone who understands the social oppression minorities face, I reply, "Yes, but you still benefit from the system that oppresses minorities." So, no Mom, I'm not ashamed that you and Dad and Tony served in the military, because you all made choices based on what you thought was best for yourselves at the time based on the lies sold to you. You all sold your youth, and Tony buried his Marine buddies to unknowingly serve imperialism so someone else could make a buck. Maybe you all realized it, maybe you still don't but I don't resent you in any way for joining the military. I am proud to be your son.

I am, however, currently outraged about the 75-year-long occupation in Palestine, and the active genocides occurring all over the world, wars started in the name of "Democracy", and the West's complicity AND PARTICIPATION in all of it. I am ashamed of living in a land that is so ashamed of its true history that it tries to whitewash it and pretend it never existed.

The media has brainwashed 98% of Americans into talking about the NFL, Taylor Swift, or their Spring Break plans, instead of how our value as humans is being extracted every day while we wander on this big tax farm to serve the elites in their ridiculous wars while simultaneously burning this planet to the point that nothing can inhabit it. No one born before the millennials wants to come to terms with these truths because they have too much invested in it. The media will have you, me, and everyone else thinking that people who share my beliefs are crazy, but these are the most important issues in the world right now. If this project is truly about shining the light of empathy, then it has to be shown here as well.

As Ryan's parents, we want to help him navigate the world in a way that is meaningful to everyone because he has incredible gifts to share. If you ask other parents of those born in 2001—oddly the year our country was attacked and would be forever changed—those parents will also likely tell you that their young adults are struggling. I come back to the prevalence of the "human condition," and I know that as alone as he feels at this time, he is in good company.

The data is overwhelming, and the cards are stacked against Generation Z. According to the National Institute of Mental Health, 33.7% of males 18-25 have a mental illness which is defined as a mental, behavioral, or emotional disorder.[22] His demographic has one of the highest rates of mental illness, and it's easy to understand why when you take into consideration all the obstacles they have to happiness and launching. But my son... he doesn't merely want to be happy. He wants liberty, freedom, and equality for others.

Because of mental illness and financial obstacles to moving out, nearly 56% of men aged 18-24 still live with their parents.[23] This reality that many young people find themselves in can be alienating, and embarrassing, and it lowers their self-esteem. Young people are in trouble, and so is our future as a nation if we can't figure out a way to empathize, understand, and help them.

---

22 *National Institute of Mental Health. (2023, March). Mental illness. Retrieved February 3, 2024, from National Institute of Mental Health website: https://www.nimh.nih.gov/health/statistics/mental-illness.*

23 *Woolfe, S. (2018, July 12). Living with Your Parents as an Adult and Your Self-Esteem | Healthy Place. Retrieved February 3, 2024, from www.healthyplace.com website: https://www.healthyplace.com/blogs/buildingselfesteem/2018/7/living-with-your-parents-as-an-adult-and-your-self-esteem.*

Getting involved in a local church is a great solution because places of worship offer social belonging and activities that enrich people's lives, as well as meaningful connections, and opportunities to give back to the community. But what if your young adult, like our son, is agnostic? For Ryan, "the Bible contains too many contradictions, and the flock is too hypocritical." Church is not a realistic resource for connection and mentoring for everyone. It just isn't.

So where do we go from here? How do we help our young people who are lost to become productive members of society? They need a purpose-driven, deliberate intervention to bring meaningful connections socially and professionally into their windshield so that they assimilate into society in each of their unique and beautiful ways. This generation does not need to be ostracized but celebrated for their resilience and incredible potential. Despite the bleak picture I have painted of Ryan's current challenges, I can assure you that his ability to do good and leave a deeply valuable mark on the world is wildly apparent whenever you are in his presence.

We must find a way, as a society, to recognize an entire generation's best stuff may go untapped because we don't empathize or understand them. Parents like Tony and I have done everything we can do to raise these young people. We have survived a pandemic, we love our kids, and we have done the very best for them. Most of us are also exhausted from the constant worry for our children growing up in this toxic world. We need help. We need our village.

They need mentors. It's not a new concept. Mentoring originated from the poem Odyssey, written around the 12th century BC by Homer.[24] Mentoring with well-defined rules and boundaries is

24 *Mentoring Origin, Types & Benefits. (2022). Retrieved February*

the most effective way of impacting a young person, and a parent cannot be a mentor.

Formal mentoring programs organized by employers, or more specifically, human resource managers, can be the catalyst our world needs right now. Matching is done by managers, software, or by self-matching. Once they are paired up, the mentor and mentee follow a set schedule to meet regularly to discuss and handle issues affecting the mentee.

In the context of a mentoring relationship, the two individuals form a caring relationship, and they collaborate and set realistic goals to keep the mentee on track to reach them. The mentor offers practical advice, stories on how they have handled similar issues, and they offer practical resources and referrals that will help the mentee get past their challenges.

The effects of a successful mentorship program are individual and collectively felt, launching the organization which invests in it the potential of exponential growth, improving communities, families, and our future ability to rise to the demands of an increasingly competitive global economy. And here's the magical part, eventually the mentee outgrows the mentor because they build the life skills they need to get past their challenges on their own. Mentees become future mentors and the cycle of goodness repeats itself.

Furthermore, the rewards felt by the mentor are also pivotal, including learning new technology skills, improved leadership skills, and boosted confidence. Let us not minimize the feeling one gets from helping another. It's a great feeling and one we

3, 2024, from Study.com website: https://study.com/academy/lesson/history-of-mentoring.html.

need more often today as so many of us are hopeless for the future and don't know where to invest our energies.

But mentoring is a profound way to help just one person and it has the power to change the world. Building hope in hopeless individuals may be the most profound way that we in organizational leadership can demonstrate empathy, and by investing in the creation and facilitation of mentorship programs corporately and as individual mentors, we can save this lost generation. It's an exciting proposition and one I hope is one that will be embraced by all leaders in the future.

Remember our friend, Dr Jansen? She believes in the power of mentorship as a pathway toward humanization by building empathy. "Humanization emerges as a dynamic and vitalizing force within the fabric of our societal interactions. It constitutes the very essence through which individuals coexist and undergo collective development. This phenomenon, characterized by its dynamic and emerging nature, facilitates and serves as a catalyst for individual and communal wellness and maturation."[25]

Jansen continues by sharing what she learned as a professional coach for the past two decades and by interviewing several individuals from the Human Library in Copenhagen. As leaders, the practice of making a conscious effort toward the humanization of others through practical programs such as mentoring can provide a "framework for nurturing growth as a cohesive living organism."

25 *LauraLynn, Jansen,. "Moksa, Seeking a Humanizing Way of Being: I Am Recognized. I Am Acknowledged. I Am Human." AURA - Antioch University Repository and Archive, 2023, aura. antioch.edu/ etds/978. Accessed 12 Dec. 2023.*

Jansen goes onto profess that seeking to help others uncover their humanity is core to how as a collective entity we can acknowledge and honor each person's individuality. By maintaining focus on both the individual's and the community's well-being, humanization assumes a pivotal role in shaping and sustaining the intricate interplay of being human."

So many people today are kind, but they are also too busy, too selfish, and too pride filled to want or to know how to help. Ultimately the challenge toward changing the world feels too vast of a problem for individuals to tackle. That's why as leaders, our impact can be further reaching. Humanization then presents an opportunity on a corporate level. But here is the issue; so many are not ready.

Jansen explains a barrier to change in this profound way: "In our modern culture, there is a wave of privilege, producing a significant imbalance. The separation of self from another can generate a dangerous sense of entitlement, making us content, selfish, and ignorant. In the business world, this sense of power separates the notion of self and one's organization from environmental and societal impact. In any circumstance, such a stance of privilege over another causes a disregard or amnesia for the advantage one beholds. These factors are building a world of disconnection and individualization."[26]

Now, here are the results of this wave of privilege that has swept over us. According to the Society of Human Resource Management (SHRM), nearly half of employees (49 percent) have thought about leaving their current organization, while

---

26 *LauraLynn, Jansen,. "Moksa, Seeking a Humanizing Way of Being: I Am Recognized. I Am Acknowledged. I Am Human." AURA - Antioch University Repository and Archive, 2023, aura. antioch.edu/ etds/978. Accessed 12 Dec. 2023.*

nearly one in five have left a job due to culture in the past five years.[27]

I believe change will come when everyone starts listening to their own small, quiet voice. Then we can turn the epidemic of being miserable at work into something of the past because people will be excited to come to work again. "Billions of wasted dollars. Millions of miserable people. It's not a war zone—it's the state of the American workplace," said SHRM president and CEO Johnny C. Taylor, Jr., SHRM-SCP.[25]

27 *SHRM Reports Toxic Workplace Cultures Cost Billions. (2019, September 25). Retrieved February 3, 2024, from www.shrm.org website: https://www.shrm.org/about/press-room/shrm-reports-toxic-workplace-cultures-cost-billions.*

CHAPTER 13

IT IS TIME TO RETHINK THE AMERICAN DREAM

On April 20th I was having serious issues working for the company I had been employed at for the past six years. Although I worked from home their control over me became unwelcome and whenever I took a call or attended a meeting others could tell that I was agitated. I continued like this for several months hoping it would change on its own. Attending the Fierce Gala should have been a way for me to connect with my coworkers and improve my morale, but it had the opposite effect and now I was completely exasperated. As I was the director of marketing, it was my job to steadfastly promote the organization, its individual apartment communities, and ultimately the people who provided those services.

My job performance depended on my ability to do this every day in every task I completed. I also answered all the surveys and reviews that came through Google, Facebook, Yelp, or Apartment Ratings. I assisted the human resources department by facilitating our employee of the month program, by creating job ads on local sites, and by promoting the company as a great place to work. Another part of my role as marketing director that I relished was shopping, evaluating, and implementing new systems and software that made it easier for our employees to do their jobs and to better serve our residents. Usually, my ideas were met by deaf ears, so improvement didn't happen. "It's too expensive," was generally their reason... if I got one at all.

We lost our competitive edge in the communities we serve because our competition was paying to implement many of these new processes, despite the cost. I saw this disparity as the leadership's disregard for our employees' contributions. How could we continue to compete under these circumstances? I was doomed to fail.

The constant revolving door of good people being hired and resigning when they realized they had been baited and hooked was the ultimate red flag for me. They hired a recruiter to fill vacancies and blamed COVID-19 for the lack of qualified and willing new employees. For years, I begged the leadership to hire a consultant to institute real and lasting change, but they were too proud to ask for help and things were only getting worse.

Good employees were resigning, and our investors and residents were noticing the constant turnover. It was not a good look for the company, so they used "current trends," human resources, and marketing as their scapegoats. On that Thursday, I was having a particularly difficult time breathing and having panic attacks about what I had to do each day because as the ultimate proponent for our company, I no longer believed in them. I was no longer in line with my ethical compass when I sat in my office chair. I had never had panic attacks before, so this was an unusual day.

By now you have likely ascertained that I am a completely transparent person, not to mention, expressive. So, on this day, I decided to let my pen do the talking so that I could completely communicate the complexity of my feelings and the situations facing the marketing department. It was a long overdue email in which I asked for weekly meetings with my CEO. This was something that she told me we would do when I was hired and professed to understand the importance of on the rare occasions that I got a formal review.

In my last email to the boss, I also alerted her to what I saw to be cultural flaws and I offered several practical remedies. Some of these solutions were software implementations and other tools that I had already emailed her about several times, but she had not been replying to my emails. Especially since the Fierce Awards, it seemed as if my CEO was pushing me out with her apathy regarding everything that I thought was important.

In my epic, last email to my boss I also asked my CEO for follow-up about projects I was working on over the past several weeks. I told her that I felt completely unsupported at work. I also shared what I was going through with my husband's health, and the challenges I was facing with my son, who may or may not graduate high school in the next month. At this point, the school was not calling us back so I thought that it could go either way. I was even so brave as to tell her about the challenges I was having representing a company that didn't listen to their employees and one that had such a high turnover.

"Why was it like this?" I had asked her to consider, but she was a proud woman and saw no issues in her ranks. I was the problem because I was the one trying to fix things. But one cannot fix what they do not recognize as broken. That was the problem.

In my six years working for this company, I had rarely, if ever taken a sick day, and at this point, I had over one hundred hours of PTO on the books, but taking time off meant more work when I got back to the office. It meant things would fall apart in my absence. Most of the upper management had the same challenges so most of us just didn't take vacations. It wasn't worth it.

PTO abuse was very common among upper management at my company, and it overwhelmed all of us. Because of the breadth of my workload, because I had no one to delegate my duties to, and because my company operated in a constant state of putting out fires instead of trying to be proactive, my coworkers and contractors had to call me when I was off.

Enjoying my vacation days was impossible, and because I had used my days off, not for fun, but to run errands and improve my mental health, the interruptions I had recently experienced while I was off were even more insulting. Those tasks were still pending, and I was still overwhelmed with life, so I asked to take the following week off.

The email took me all afternoon to write but I didn't care. This was important. My husband had cancer; I was having an existential crisis. I know that I overshared and vented, in my last email to the boss but I did so professionally. I was trying to appeal to her human side and at this point... I figured that I had nothing to lose. I signed my email in my customary fashion, "All the Best," and I hit send and waited for the fallout.

My CEO responded and denied my request to take next week off. I forwarded her reply and my email to our HR manager who was sick at home, but she answered her email anyway and she granted my vacation. I would take a week off, gather my thoughts, figure out what I wanted, and deal with all this work stuff when I got back. I was really in no shape to make any decisions right now anyway.

I returned from my week with a clear head. I would indeed resign, but the problem was, I didn't have another job yet. That was stressing me out. How could I resign and expect my husband with cancer to support us? The night before I would send my resignation to HR it became impossible for me to breathe. I already had high blood pressure, but that night the anxiety and panic attacks took me down, but Tony was there to pick me up off the floor. "I've got you," he said. I was sobbing uncontrollably at this point, and I said in between gasps, "But you have CANCER. Who's got you?" Then, my Amazing Man said something that calmed me for the first time in four months. "I've got me too, babe. I can handle this. Resign."

I had successfully journaled for thirty days and traveled to learn about who I was at this new point in my life, all while working full-time. I embraced the lessons that I learned, make that, earned. I had sought out help from friends, confidants, and professionals and I was ready to see what I could do if I let go. The process had already been so cathartic, but I think what helped me more than anything has been knowing that the lessons I learned while writing it all down may actually help others. Perhaps, my lessons and the effort it has taken to write it all down will have the power to change the world. I had to at least try. It's the deal I made with the universe on May 2nd, when I jumped off the hamster wheel.

During the first two weeks of my writing journey, it became clear that my journal would become a book because the concepts I uncovered are important to shine a light upon. At the end of those first thirty days of writing—and the lessons I learned along the way—I was no longer sensing discouragement from my Small, Quiet Voice, and I had set new priorities.

When those thirty days of introspection were over, I was a new person emotionally, philosophically, and physically. I also wrote my business plan for my consultancy firm and committed myself to a new professional path in organizational leadership.

SATURDAY, APRIL 22, 2023 – 1:20 PM

At the Honda Dealership

My car needs an oil change so here I sit. Despite my boss's denial for me to take vacation hours next week, my human resources manager pushed it through. Perhaps my mention of "cancer" had something to do with it? So, it looks like I'm going to have some time for mental health after all. One thing I realized yesterday as I was scrambling with all our vendors to make sure they could cover me next week, is that when these people found out that I was finally taking a few days off they all said, "Have fun!" These colleagues and contractors that I have been working with for six years… they sincerely meant that I deserved to go have some fun, and they didn't say it as a nicety.

But this is the only dialogue that we have regarding work-life balance in this country. Why? Just that expression of "have fun," as you're on your way out the door is the only mention that vacations get in corporate America. But taking and actually enjoying your PTO is so important to your mental health. Why aren't we talking about this more? The work-life balance conversation is not being brought to light and it needs to be talked about, examined, and analyzed for the cherished thing that vacations should be to all Americans.

The topic certainly needs to be much higher on the list of priorities for all of us, especially HR and leaders within our organizations. Doctors are so keen to write a prescription for anti-depressants when what they should be asking instead is, "How long has it been since you have been on a real vacation?" People in this country are fried. The culture needs to be fixed.

That's the reason why I created PTOAffirm, a program that works to fix this problem and benefit organizations that commit to its promises. It's an easy thing to do but it will have lasting and meaningful results.[28]

The Oxford English Dictionary defines the American dream as "the ideal that every citizen of the United States should have an equal opportunity to achieve success and prosperity through hard work, determination, and initiative." It is literally written into our code as Americans that you will burn out. It sounds more like the American Nightmare. Our society needs to realize that people are what makes the world run, not the accomplishment of tasks. It's time to rethink the American Dream.

"Another world is not only possible; she is on her way. On a quiet day I can hear her breathing."

Arundhati Roy

I don't have any fun planned for next week yet. Not really, but I desperately need fun. Maybe it will help me when I go back to work next Monday. I hope I will have a smile on my face and not want to scratch everyone's eyes out when I get back to work. In trying to plan my week off, my next big adventure, I had some intriguing Facebook conversations with Corinne Foster about a Facebook post she recently made about converting her ring, and her husband's ring into something artistic and special. She just moved from Colorado to Cocoa Beach, and she lost her husband about five years ago. Since then, her posts dealing with the grief of losing him have really inspired me. I haven't seen Corinne since the early nineties, but she has always been part of the youth-gone-wild crew.

28 *PTOAffirm, www.ptoaffirm.com, www.ptoaffirm.com. Accessed 12 Dec. 2023.*

This feels like when I was going through my divorce with Elijah. I'm excavating my former self with urgency and passion, and this time I don't want a divorce, but I do need things to change. New boundaries need to be established for me to continue. I'm tired of cooking all the meals, and cleaning up after the boys and Tony, and I am most tired of nagging them to ask for their help. These are household chores, and they are part of the household. Everyone pitches in. Isn't that how I raised these boys? I don't want to do it anymore.

It's happening again. The waves are pushing me toward more lessons from mermaids that I knew, and I loved from long ago. I'm good at making friends, just a typical Leo. People know this about me. I'm kind of famous for it. I have also always believed that the universe sends friends into my life at certain times when they need me, just as I need them.

The exchange of mermaid wisdom is not always in equal measure because of the cycles of our lives, but as others invest their energy, we reciprocate the best we can. It is a beautiful exchange that has always inspired me. The universe has sent me so many friends throughout the years, and they have taught me so much and loved me so hard. Those interactions have brought out different parts of me. I am so thankful and contemplative now because I have shared life with all these different people.

My mermaids have taught me how to love, how to live, and how to make better decisions. They have taught me how to celebrate victories, how to accept defeat, and how to breathe in the storm. They are my chosen family. As I have been planning my trip along the east coast of Florida, I have become more and more curious about what special lessons I might take away from these new experiences, places, people, and things. I will watch and listen intently to it all. The last time I left town was three weeks ago. At that time, I was running away from something, and I wasn't sure of anything. But this time I'm running toward so much love and I know exactly what I want for my future.

I have made a list and I have people in my life that are helping me realize it. I feel so much better about where Tony and I are at in our marriage right now. I'm in a much better head space. I can see clearly, and I know exactly what I need to do. Let the surfing reconvene!

I am leaving tomorrow, and I will see Sadie Jones, my old friend from our Air Force days back in Spokane. I haven't seen her since 2000 when we both got out of the military. Thank goodness for Facebook or I would have lost track of her. I decided to try to make it a surprise and coordinate with her husband through Facebook Messenger. I can't wait to meet him and their four-year-old little boy, who was conceived after thousands of dollars' worth of IVF. He's a true miracle and he looks like a firecracker.

James, her husband, seems like a cool person too. I know he had a stroke when Sadie was pregnant so I'm curious to see how he's doing. I'm sure he's amazing. Then I will get to spend the night with my old friend from Laughlin Insurance, Jen's couch. From Jen and Ron's at Satellite Beach, I will head to Cocoa Beach to spend some time with Corrine. I will get to reconnect with my old high school buddy.

Back in 1990, she moved into my mom and stepdad's house with me for two weeks before graduation. I couldn't remember the reason she stayed with us, but I do remember there was some drama at home and that we had an extra bed. The last stop on my trip will be with my new friend, Liz, who had already invited me to meet her in Fort Lauderdale on Thursday while we were at the Indigo Girls concert last week.

Liz originally wanted to drive to Fort Lauderdale from Tampa together, but because of my last-minute travel plans, I will just meet her there. I met Liz, an empowered single mom and entrepreneur, recently through a mutual friend who now lives in Maine. We all had brunch together in Safety Harbor and had a tremendous time, laughing, catching up, and wandering around the farmers market, as women do. This place, its energy and it's vibrant storefronts, and rich native American and colonial history. I love calling it home.

Liz made a sincere effort to keep in touch with me after that first meeting. She was trying intentionally to be a good friend to me. She barely knew me, but Liz understood that I was having a tough time with the cancer diagnosis, so she invited me to a concert at Ruth Ekhard Hall, less than a mile from our house. She and I had way too much fun at the concert, and our next plan together was a Fort Lauderdale trip to pick up her son from college. When I asked her, via text, if it would be okay if we took separate cars and just met up there, she replied, "Whatever you need lady. I got you."

As I left my other mermaids in my rear-view mirror and Fort Lauderdale got closer, I started thinking that this final leg of my thirty-day journaling pilgrimage needed to end in a special way. I didn't want to keep on writing all my thoughts down and these thirty days seemed to have taught me enough. I was ready to move onto the next stage of our life, lessons learned, and outlined and ready to be expounded on at a later day.

So, with the adventure behind me, before I could leave Fort Lauderdale, I made a detour. I needed to get a tattoo. When I was still in Cocoa Beach I pulled over, and googled "mermaid wave tattoo," and the first image that popped up was perfect. The non-originality of the design was perhaps what I enjoyed the most. It was as if I was getting a symbol that stood for more than just my own experiences. Perhaps I was getting a tattoo that any woman might at one time in her life fully understand.

The next day as I exited "The Venice of America," I stopped at a walk-in studio and had the inside of my left wrist marked with the image I had pulled up on Google. It became a promise to myself that I would never again work for another organization that didn't align with my own principles. The act of getting that tattoo was incredibly personal and empowering.

CHAPTER 13

MOMMING

All my mother ever wanted to do was raise children, and she was really good at it. I remember as a young girl, I never wanted for anything. She had this magical way of finding thrift store clothes that were adorable and she had the ability to stretch our frugal grocery budget to make delicious and healthy meals. As far as I knew, my sister Brianne, my mom, and I were just like every other family.

She received seventy-five dollars each month in child support from our dad, she qualified for food stamps and welfare, and we just always miraculously got by on what she could figure out. My mom was also resourceful and persuasive, and she knew how to hustle. So much so that she convinced our landlords who lived in the house above our basement apartment to let her insulate a corner of the garage so she could have a stained-glass studio to make huge windows for the affluent people who owned big houses down on the Yampa River.

Then, when that work was slow, she started patching the knees of men's jeans who worked at the power plant outside of town. It would seem Mom found a lucrative niche for the hard-working men that lived in our town, as it was indeed more affordable to pay five dollars to add knee patches to a pair of jeans than to buy a new pair an replace them. Coincidentally, that's how she met my stepdad, too. Well, that and a healthy serving of homemade stew. She always said that food was the way to a man's heart. That's probably why I wanted to learn how to cook like her. Being an excellent cook was always an integral part of being a woman, a wife, and a mom.

The happiest memories of my childhood were in our one-bedroom basement apartment on the top of Legion Street. Mom had the bedroom with the door, and Brianne and I each had single beds behind the couch. Mom had fashioned a room divider from a colorful printed sheet that she hung down the middle of the living room behind the couch to block the sun from waking us up in the morning.

The living room was essentially cut into three sections by her design with the space opposite my mom's room in front of the bathroom serving as a sitting area i.e., a stage. This is where Brianne and I would perform for family and friends whenever they would come over for a visit. Our favorite songs to sing along to or to lip sync included The Oakridge Boys', *Elvira*, or anything from the *Sing Along Songs for Kids* album my mom had picked up at a yard sale.

When we were only four and seven and too young to venture down the alley, or out front, we would play in the backyard with the landlord's chocolate lab. On the north side of the property, there was a natural slope, rustically landscaped with shrubs and boulders. That hill became our pirate hide-out or a deserted island, and sometimes another planet if we could get our hands on a cardboard box that we could make into a rocket ship. My sister and I would play outside all day and get into mischief. Mom would make us homemade popsicles and bring them out in the afternoon, all varieties of juice, including orange, lemon, grape, or apple. She even experimented with a savory tomato juice with peas popsicle that we liked.

My mom was the queen of domestic frugality, and everyone knew it. One summer afternoon, as Brianne and I were lost in pretend play, I brought a pair of scissors outside to equip my beauty shop. My only customer that day was my little sister and we decided that a drastic change was needed to reach her most glamorous potential. That was the day that I cut Brianne's beautiful waist-length hair off into a punk-rock, short bob. My mom was disappointed in me, but I don't remember being reprimanded because I was so young, and really... I was just pretending anyway.

My mother made our lives magical, and she did it effortlessly... or at least that was the way it seemed. She told everyone who asked about her decision not to go back to work, "I am not going to let anyone else raise my children. They are my girls and I want this time with them." That bold principle was one she got from her own mother who had also been a stay-at-home mom, as most women were in that generation. But because of mom's commitment to stay home with us and her lack of a husband, money was always tight.

I remember that she hung a parchment scripted in cursive calligraphy in a gold frame that said, "Please, No Smoking. Tiny Lungs at Work," and she never allowed anyone to pollute our lungs in our house, although when we were at our dad's every other weekend, second-hand smoke was something we had to endure.

We didn't have a car, so my paternal grandma—her best friend —would drive us to the store for the weekly shopping trip. Mom was a happy woman, and she loved her girls more than life itself. There was nothing she wouldn't do for my sister and me, and we both knew it. She taught us determination and how to laugh at ourselves, how to tell time, and right from wrong. There was never a better mom in the history of moms, and she was fulfilled by being a mother. I thought she didn't work, but I can remember her toiling well into the evenings and on the weekends with her side hustles. She worked, that I can assure you.

Mom had two other children ten and thirteen years after I was born, so to me it seemed like she was a mom forever. She was so good at it. But as I got older and started seeing the comparisons between other moms who worked outside the home, I started to lose respect for her choices and feel sad for her because she never got to have a professional identity, except before I was born as a dental assistant. She never really had her own money, and that part bothered me.

Because of all this, I had a strong desire to grow up to be both a good mom and have a fulfilling career. My oldest son Andrew came along when I was twenty-three and when I was nearly done with my second enlistment in the Air Force. I could have opted to get out of the military when I was pregnant, but I decided to stay in the military for another two years and be an active-duty mom. I didn't have any other choice because Elijah had already gotten out of the Air Force, and he didn't have a decent job in the civilian sector. We needed my consistent paycheck to keep the lights on and pay our mortgage.

I did not have the option to stay at home with Andrew, but I had good friends who had given birth while in the military and they had found ways to manage it all, so I learned lessons from them. What I discovered was that the Air Force was very accommodating to a young mom's needs for pumping milk, taking extra time off at lunch to go see your baby, and limiting the stress on young moms so they could cope with being a parent. There were services on base for new moms and an excellent Child Development Center for daycare, so I felt supported by my community.

As soon as I got out of the Air Force in 2000 when Andrew was two, I started selling Pampered Chef. Then Ryan was born in 2001 and I started working as an ad executive about a year later. Finally, Ethan came along in 2004, and when we did the math, we realized that I couldn't make enough to pay for daycare, so I stayed home and went back to school. I struggled at home with him as a baby. While our first two sons were so easy, Ethan cried all the time unless I was holding him or nursing him. It was constant parenting, and I had two other boys to care for. I reasoned that I needed to go back to work then, or I risked my sanity.

He was a wonderful baby and I love Ethan so much, but he demanded all of my energy, and it was exhausting. He wasn't like that with anyone else though and did so well in the care of others, so I took a job at Safeco Insurance call center for about a year. It was an excellent company and I made friends and developed my sales skills there. I could develop rapport and cross-sell policies better than anyone on the sales floor and I won awards for it.

Like my mom, I stayed home with my boys and had my side hustles for about seven years, off and on. I worked when I needed to, applied for WIC, and found niches I could fulfill to make extra money, but I also found the time to earn my degree because I sincerely believe that education is the pathway to success. I strived to do more and be more for my kids. Most of the time I was okay with all of this, but many days balancing it all left me zapped.

My scenario begs the age-old feminist question, "Can women truly have it all?" Now that my youngest is getting ready to graduate high school, I realize that my kids don't need me anymore. There were a lot of sacrifices that I made to be a mom over the years, and there were big ones that Tony made too to be with me. There were challenges for sure, but the rewards were far greater.

Even through poverty, divorce, and Elijah's alcoholism, I don't regret anything about becoming a mom. Over the past 25 years, Elijah and I, as well as our Amazing Man, have balanced it all and raised three amazing men. We love the boys so much, and I love that our family has been pieced together by finding balance in the sacrifice.

But the small voice inside that had been whispering for my entire adult life started screaming at me when Tony got diagnosed with cancer. "If not now, WHEN? Get on with fulfilling your destiny NOW! If you don't do it NOW, you will never get another opportunity!"

Looking back on my life I realize that I have been blessed by being all these things to so many people along the way. I have had diverse and unique experiences and met so many unforgettable characters. I also know now that I have been taking notes throughout my entire life so that I could write this book for you.

The kids aren't even out of the house yet and I'm already manifesting all this creativity. I'm still working, for God's sake, and I'm finding time on walks and on drives at night when I should be sleeping to get this out of me. It's not a baby because I don't want to nurse my book after it comes out. This book is also not an egg, because I'm not going to sit on it and wait, as a hen would. No, in truth, *You Have Arrived* is more like a baby frog or a fish that has sprung out of me. Yes, I like the analogy of a frog the best. I love frogs. Yes, I am a momma frog that has been swimming around for a long time, and at this point, I am just so full of life, that at this point I must release some back into the world. I am also thankfully, in a safe place right now. Now is the best time to finally release all these busy and full eggs into the stream. I have arrived.

I wanted a glimpse inside Sadie's life this week and it's been wonderful. Her little boy is perfect in every way. He is exuberant, mannered, funny, and intelligent, and Sadie is an excellent mother, just like I always knew she would be. After the stroke, James is half of what he used to be physically, and socially. He is also verbally challenged, which I can see is very discouraging for a man's man like him. He seems to take it all in stride though, and he's just thankful to be alive.

James suffered a brain hemorrhage when Sadie was pregnant, and he nearly died. But he came out of the coma to be a dad and a husband for his family. The emotional toll of that time has left its mark on my friend. Sure, when he came home, James was a different person, but now nearly five years after the stroke, Sadie remains committed to him.

She wears her wedding ring even though they're not legally married. That detail has not yet been realized because they spent their money on IVF instead. Sadie told me that she does not need sex, and she does not need anything from anyone else. Their relationship is different than they thought it would be, but the three of them are living their best lives together in the way that works for them, and they are thankful. It was a beautiful thing to witness.

I encouraged my sweet friend, and I loved on her, and we sang some old songs together. Sadie has not changed over the years. She is still the same beautiful woman; independent, fierce, and caring. I'm so proud to be her friend.

Now on to see Jen, my pal from my days at Laughlin Insurance back in Panama City over a decade ago. That time in my life was challenging because at any time anyone could walk in from off the street and ask for anything, but after they left, we could always have a good laugh about what had just transpired.

Because we were dealing with the chaos that comes with customer service, there was always so much to talk about. While we worked together over that year, we spoke about the injustices of the world, and we realized that our morality meters were set at the same level.

She and I became kindred spirits then, and because of that, it has always been very comfortable to hang out with Jen and her sweet husband, Ron. As I was driving the two hours to see her, Jen was at a big doctor's appointment. Over the past few years, her lupus had caused damage to her spleen and liver, and today she would find out how much damage had been done.

She texted me earlier in the day and said for the past two years that she hadn't been able to get the medicine her doctors said she needed to keep her body in balance. It was a medication I had heard of in the news called Ivermectin, and it was now out of stock because fanatics were taking it during the pandemic. She had not been able to get this life-saving medicine she needed for way too long, and now she had confirmation that lupus had taken a serious toll on her spleen and her liver. She was sick. We met up at a Mexican restaurant for a late lunch to catch up so that Jen could report to her husband and me what the doctor had told her. When Jen ducked out to the bathroom, I asked Ron what blood type she was, to which he replied, "I think O-negative."

I told him that Jen and I had the same blood type and that if Jen needed some of my liver, I would donate a piece to her. Am I that good of a friend? Am I that brave or stupid to give a piece of me to a friend in need? Jen and I talked about it, and I told her I was serious about my offer. She and I joked that we could get matching mermaid tattoos if the transplant had to happen.

At this point in my journey, I had never gotten a tattoo, but she had a few, and so did most of my family. Andrew has them and so do my four siblings: masterpieces up and down their arms, or in other more intimate places on their torso. Their bodies represented a gallery of original and traditional tattoo art from wise artists. I love to hear the stories of why anyone gets a tattoo to commemorate a lost loved one or pet, as a tribute to their battles, or as recognition over victories won, but the symbolism has always been lost on me. Nothing was ever that important or meaningful, or maybe I just never took the time out to think about it.

CHAPTER 15

TOM BODELL SAID HE'D LEAVE THE LIGHT ON FOR YOU (But We'll Kick You Out at Eleven)

THURSDAY, APRIL 27TH, 2023, 10:46 AM

At the Motel 6 at Cocoa Beach

I woke up around nine o'clock this morning and surprisingly I had a pretty good sleep on this old mattress. While I was out with Corrine last night, she never offered to let me crash at her house. I thought that odd since she knew that I drove to Cocoa Beach to see her, and we had been pretty good friends in high school.

She just said that her eighteen-year-old son is choosing to be miserable, and that their home was not a good place for guests right now. Corrine's son was choosing to be sad, therapy had stalled, and he refused to take medication to get over his dad's death. It has been five years, and he was still in a dark cloud, and according to his mom, it was all playing out like a Greek tragedy.

Corrine has always been an interesting person and that is even more true now. She is still that fiery redhead I remember, but now there is such an aura of mystery and grief that surrounds her and it seemed to me that at any moment it might come pouring out of her. I remember meeting her in the early nineties. She was two years older than me. and we were not that close. It was a long time ago, but I have foggy memories of her at parties I attended and in the halls of our high school. She and I have several mutual friends, now on Facebook, as we did in the halls of Moffat County High School. I recall that she always made me feel comfortable when I spoke to her… and she still has that way about her.

That's why it surprised me when she told me over drinks tonight, she had no memories of me from our youth. We have been friends on Facebook for several years, and that is the only way she knows me. But then she told me that she does not only have any memories of me, but she has virtually no memories of her entire high school career.

She says the reason for her amnesia is that she drank a lot during those years. When I told her that she and I had been good enough friends for her to stay at my house for the last two weeks of high school, before she graduated, she looked at me like a deer in the headlights. She honestly didn't remember getting ready for school, driving to school together, or putting her graduation gown on at my house back in 1991.

She fought with her parents and needed a place to stay, and my parents were okay with it for a little while. I told her a couple of stories I remembered vividly about that time in our lives together, but she didn't remember them. It made me sad, but if that was her truth there is nothing that I could do to change that. Our insignificant and long-lost friendship slipped away from her years ago. I was just a casual acquaintance to her now, and she didn't trust me.

She and I met up at a beach bar and restaurant like so many others I had been to over the years while living in Florida, called Coconuts on the Beach. My GPS was so confused. The bar was located behind a one-way street alongside several other buildings within a quadrant, and I could find no parking. Just a lot of weird one-way streets. Needless to say, Coconuts was hard to find, but I think the oddities of Cocoa Beach are also part of its charm. I was rolling with it.

Once I got there and checked the place out, I was enamored by it. I waited at the bar for Corrine and when she arrived, we had a shot of (good) tequila to commemorate this occasion. Then she and I shared a nice meal on the back deck overlooking the ocean. A black cat nearly hopped onto our table. It seemed that Mr. Puss lived at Coconuts and according to three members of their waitstaff, who all said it at the same time, "he eats better than you do."

Our waiter was a sweet guy. He came up to chit-chat and build rapport. He was doing his job. He was a chucklehead and said, "The best tip that I ever got, I got from that table right there." He pointed to the other two ladies in the booth adjacent to us, pulled out his phone, and showed us all an adorable photo of a chubby black pup. As if on cue, all four of us ladies within earshot let out an audible, "Awe!" The waiter explained that he had been chit-chatting with a couple two years ago who was sitting in that booth, and they gave him a black Labrador puppy as a tip. The server then showed us a photo of the mature dog and asked to see one of my dog, Stella, to which I obliged with three or four snapshots.

He smiled, shook his head, and said, “This dog saved my life. I have lost one hundred pounds since I got him.” Then Jason said something else as he left our table that I have repeated many times since then. “Dogs are too good for us. We don’t deserve them,” and he was right. Jason warmed my heart and made me think of all the good dogs I have known over the years... and for that, he got a nice, fat tip.

“Knock-Knock... Housekeeping.” I jumped. “What in the holy onomatopoeia did I just write? What is that knocking? Who could that possibly be? Oh ya... housekeeping, she said that. Sure, that makes sense. I am in a motel and it’s morning. I will just ask the nice lady if I can get a late checkout, and I am sure she will grant me a couple more hours to write in peace. The hotel is modest, but it is clean and cool enough between bursts on that old air conditioner. This place is old, but I can deal with it.

I just need a couple of hours to hang out and await Liz’s text that her workday is ending, then she will drive the three hours from her house in Tampa, south and east to Fort Lauderdale, and then I will drive three hours directly down the peninsula of Florida from Cocoa Beach to Fort Lauderdale to meet up with her for a fancy meal with her son and his friend. We plan to bond and get to know each other a little better in our suite at the Double Tree overlooking the yacht traffic through Coral Bay. I have the champagne packed and chilled.

I just want to hang out for another hour, maybe two...and keep writing I am in a flow. When I called the front desk to ask for a late check out, the not-so-friendly-woman told me that housekeeping is on her way down the hall, and she will be at my room soon, and that I need to check out now. “Oh my gosh, what time is it?” I ask, fully knowing it’s close to eleven.

You are probably wondering why I chose that seedy motel when I could have afforded a nicer room. For one, I wanted the experience of that old Cocoa Beach style of Americana, and boy did The Motel 6 deliver! I would learn later that night on the phone with Tony that he used to hang out there in the early nineties. He had come to Florida to follow his dream of playing minor-league baseball. He had a girlfriend in Satellite Beach and followed her to Gainesville after he injured his shoulder. This area had been his home and was steeped in memories of his youth. I wondered if that was why he never wanted to take me to the east coast of Florida.

I heard the cart rolling down the corridor, so I knew she was coming. I threw on a comfy dress, collected all my things and scurried down the stairs to my car to check out of Tom Bodett's place. It would seem that they did not do late check outs here. I needed to find another place to sit and write today while I waited for the next leg of my journey to happen.

CHAPTER 16

FINDING JOY

As I type this, my bracelets are digging into my arms and my back is in spasm. It is time to get up and stretch and evaluate ergonomics. The keyboard is too far away from my body and I am hunched over; my legs are crossed. This chair has no lumbar support. After I stand up and sway from side to side for a few times on my Oofos and stretch my arms over my head, it occurs to me that I have been so intent on writing over the past four hours that I have been ignoring this ever-increasing pain for at least the last hour.

This reminds me of when I was in labor with the boys. Eventually the contractions got so strong that I couldn't sleep through them. Eventually the squeeze and pain would wake me up, and I would have to get up and deal with what was happening with my body. I was sitting in Starbucks writing and thinking about the night before and processing the next thing that I should write about in my book, chronologically after I arrived at Tom Bodett's place at around nine o'clock.

I was thankful to be somewhere quiet and safe so early in the night after going out with Corrine. I was also thankful to have found a room at all since I had not planned that night of my trip as solidly as I had all the others. So, I ended up at Motel 6 because I refused to spend more than one hundred dollars for a hotel for one night. Corrine and I had decided to pack it in early after only one drink, as Corrine's son had not been out of his room all day and she was worried about him. She did not offer me a room at her house to repay the favor from when we were young, so a cheap motel at the last minute would have to suffice.

I had sung the first song at open mic, *What's Up*, by 4 Non Blondes, and then about half an hour later, she sang two songs back-to-back, *You're No Good* by Linda Ronstadt and *White Rabbit* by Jefferson Airplane, and she did well. Those are hard songs but each time she sang, the marketer in me immediately walked to the front of the bar to record her performance. Make no mistake, neither of us were afraid to ask for permission to do anything. "I am getting some good videos for this woman." *She is really good. How did she get so good? From what I can remember, she was never in choir in school. She must have discovered her gift later in life.*

After hearing her sing, I was even more curious about Corrine's life since high school. I had noticed there were a lot of clips on her Facebook page that showed her on stage. It seemed as if her life had been a perpetual band gig before her husband Tim's death. She was happy to talk about her background as a performer, so I leaned in and listened intently.

"My late husband, Tim and I had a band together in Longmont, Colorado, for ten years." The couple and a few other friends formed a band called Tough Kitten. This was their side hustle, and during that time, Corrine described herself and Tim as strict parents raising three good kids. Life was good and the couple was working hard and enjoying all that life had to offer.

Then one afternoon in the summer of 2017, Tim was at home and was cleaning the gutters, and he fell off the ladder. There were no serious signs of injury, but his shoulder was sore. Like most men, despite the pain, he refused to go to the doctor right away. Tim had a visible bulge under his shirt that looked like his collar bone may be out of socket.

According to Corrine, the doctor they visited a few days after the accident said that Tim had just pulled a muscle and that it would heal if he wore a brace. The physician they visited was clearly not concerned (or he was off his game) when it came to diagnosing and treating this healthy, forty-one-year-old man with a painful bump near his shoulder.

Tim continued to work in some pain, but it was not constant, so neither he nor Corrine were too concerned about it. Several weeks later, the pain had mostly subsided, so Tim went elk hunting with his buddies. This is something that he and his friends, my family, and most every other family in Colorado look forward to each year. Hunting season marks the coming of fall, and it is a magical time for families to get back to nature to harvest an animal from the land. Sagebrush blooms and the aspen trees in the mountains turn from dark green to yellow. Frost covers the desert in the mornings and melts off by ten, so that hunters must shed a layer of their orange clothing in the middle of the afternoon.

This is the rhythm of life in hunting communities, and it's been that way for a hundred years. A six-hundred-pound female (cow) elk was taken down by one of the hunters and then it was quartered. Each of the four men was to lug roughly one hundred and fifty pounds of meat and bones back to camp. They were all elated and buzzing from adrenaline, knowing that the meat they harvested today would fill their freezers all year.

Although I never met Tim, I know his type. He was just like my dad and uncles, my cousins, and my grandpa. Colorado hunters love their time outdoors, communing with nature. They become recharged each fall by the tradition, the sights, smells, and above all else, the sensation they get from pulling the trigger and harvesting an elk, deer, or antelope.

The men, women, and young adults who hunt consider this their favorite time of year. They become one with the crisp air and the piercing azure skies. This is the joy of the hunt, but when the animal falls, there is also a tinge of sadness that a majestic creature has perished, but not died in vain.

There Tim was on that magnificent fall day, embracing the universe with his best friends, thanking God for his grace, and embracing all of creation. He secured the elk quarter to a rope and threw it over his shoulder, a knot in both hands to brace the weight of the meat of the animal. He was feeling joy. He was doing what he loved to do. He had found work-life balance. Tim was an entrepreneur, he was a talented musician, he was a good dad, and wonderful husband to Corrine, and during his final moments on this earth, he was enveloped by joy... then he was swept up into it.

Corrine suspects that her beloved died because of medical malpractice and that his shoulder had indeed been out of socket and gone untreated for way too long, which caused an infection and would lead to a heart attack when he exerted himself in the field that day. The nurses she later spoke with who worked at the hospital where Tim had been originally treated encouraged her to hire a lawyer, because they felt the same way she did about the case. Corrine is a strong and smart woman, and I know she will self-advocate for herself. She is a champion of what's right. She always has been... even if she does not remember.

CHAPTER 18

THE STORYTELLER

When my company burned their final bridge with me, I could have reported them to the Society of Human Resources or the National Apartment Association, but those of us who have been doing this for a while know that reporting these types of ethical infractions is difficult to impossible to prove. There really is no ethics governing board in the for-profit sector. Only ten percent of America's wage and salary workers are union members. For the rest of us, we have to deal with injustices or resign.[29]

So, instead of reporting what happened, and wasting my time, I had to do something more... something more complete, to give EVERYONE context. In other words, I had to quit my job while my husband had cancer, with zero savings in the bank, write a book, get a tattoo, and start a consulting firm to try to make a difference in the lives of others.

As you now know, that was only the first part of my journey. It turned out that I had a lot more to say about what it means to be a woman in 2023. Life is long, and it leaves many marks on us, and now, as I assess the last twelve months' journey I have been on, I believe it is a good idea to look back occasionally, to

29 *Bureau of Labor Statistics. (2022). UNION MEMBERS -2022. Retrieved from https://www.bls.gov/news.release/pdf/union2.pdf.*

see where we have been and to measure our steps against others who we admire.

We don't have to do the heavy lifting alone. Our community is out there and if you look close enough you will find them. By now you know that I got tired of playing by "their" rules and fell back on that universal, infinite truth, that the pen is mightier than the sword. Over my forty-nine years on this earth, the written word has been my best friend, my counselor, my sanctuary, my colleague, my workhorse, my megaphone, and at times my bluntest implement for revenge. When dealing with crooked bosses or unjust principles, I believe that the written word will always measure up to be far mightier than the sword.

According to National Geographic, "Some of the earliest evidence of stories comes from the cave drawings in Lascaux and Chauvet, France. The drawings, which date as far back as thirty-thousand years ago, depict animals, humans, and other objects. Some of them appear to represent visual stories."[30] Contrastingly, the first *written* word was discovered in Mesopotamia (present-day Iraq), between 3400 and 3300 BC.[31] Astoundingly, storytelling—the act of telling tales to others—and if they are important—putting them on something permanent, like a cave wall predates the written word by some two hundred and fifty thousand years!

Storytelling is at the very heart of being human because stories are fundamental to advancing societies. Shared stories represent

---

30 *Greshko, Michael. Ancient Cave Art May Depict the World's Oldest Hunting Scene. Science, 11 Dec. 2019, www.nationalgeographic.com/science/article/ancient-cave-art-inindonesia-may-be-worlds-oldest-hunting-scene. Accessed 11 Dec. 2023.*

31 *The Getty Museum. (n.d.). Retrieved December 30, 2023, from Getty Museum website: https://www.getty.edu/art/exhibitions/mesopotamia/explore.html.*

humanity's very heartbeat and its collective intelligence that was, or was not, passed on from one generation to the next. We can learn so much from stories, and we owe it to those who have offered their truth to read their stories and learn from their lessons, lest we not make the same mistakes they have made.

So, let us learn from the collective work of the rebels, the revolutionaries, the willful, and the downtrodden, and if I genuinely subscribe to the fact that our stories are fundamental to this human experience, then my story matters too. What's more, the pain and challenges, revelations, and solutions that have come out of this *storytelling experience* had to be made permanent, because not doing so would have wasted the story. This is my testimony, and it may or may not change the world, but my story might just help just one person... and that is enough.

Dear Reader, YOU are smart enough, successful enough, talented enough, good enough, beautiful enough, unique enough, bold enough, and important enough. Tell YOUR story.

CHAPTER 19

FINAL PINK FEMINIST THOUGHTS

I found it appropriate to end our journey together using the same rationale as we began, by talking about how pop culture and the art of marketing has impacted my life and that of so many others for the betterment of society.

Unless you were living under a rock in the summer of 2023, you know that this was the summer of Barbie, and for me, the message of mind twisting female ideals brought to life through our favorite childhood icon couldn't have come at a better time. Back in April when Liz and I went to see the Indigo Girls in concert and we got lost in the timeless harmonies of, *Closer I Am To Fine*, I couldn't have known that this song would be used in *Barbie* to inspire a trip into the real world of self-actualization. But I find it appropriate on so many levels that this was the song that the Greta Gerwig chose for the important and arduous task of transporting ideals into reality.[32]

There were so many other parallels between Barbie's journey of self-discovery and mine that I felt obligated to point them out for you in an effort to finalize my memoirs and leave you with a few final thoughts of wisdom. When Barbie wonders, and Billie

32 *Barbie the Movie. Directed by Greta Gerwig, Warner Bros. Pictures, 21 July 2023. https://www.barbie-themovie.com/.*

Eilish serenades us with *What Was I Made For?* is a good example. We all feel like this sometimes. I know I certainly did when I hopped in my car and headed for the beach back in late March. What I had been made for was experiencing a full range of messy emotions and learning from it. I had to press pause in order to figure that out. I realized what I was made for when I looked through a lens of optimism, friendship, and introspection. By tuning into what the world needs from us, and what we are individually, uniquely equipped to give, only then can we offer our best talents and gifts to others. This is what we were made for.

Do men really rule the world? This is neither a yes nor no answer. While Barbie marvels at how in the real world a construction site at lunchtime is not the perfect source for female encouragement, it can be noted that women have always held creative, supportive, and sometimes roles of authority that have impacted society in positive ways. In fact, women have been creating spaces, inspiring, and serving as the antagonists for ordinary men to be successful since the beginning of time. Make no bones about it, women have shaped and molded the world indirectly through their men since the dawn of time. We may not have always held the highest titles; perhaps that of mother, grandmother, sister, aunt, niece, wife, or daughter, but don't think for a minute that their contributions have not been pivotal... although great women of history rarely got the credit they deserve.

Women have managed to control the patriarchy, at least somewhat over the years. But even today if women have the same qualifications as men, most companies choose to hire the man. It makes sense. Men don't have PMS or the need to take maternity leave, and they certainly have fewer emotional outbursts. But what the patriarchy does not often consider is that those emotional and hormonal fluctuations that women experience create pathways for empathy, understanding, innovation, ingenuity, and ultimately, profitability.

Be real and be weird; be dark and crazy. Have the existential crisis or even the nervous breakdown. Just be brave enough to be you. It's so good enough. We all need to compromise and embrace diversity to be the most productive versions of ourselves so that we can lead the most competitive companies and cultivate vibrant communities. Men should resist being defined by patriarchal stereotypes and support their female colleagues' contributions because neither men nor women can do it on their own. We must work together to reach our full potential.

Here is some fierce and final advice from me and Barbie to my mermaids: you are smart, and thin, and pretty enough... I promise. Take the world by the horns and start your business, take that long-delayed vacation, have the adventure, go to the concert, and channel friendship and support from and for one another in your personal and professional pursuits. We must push aside our irrepressible thoughts of death and our insecurities about cellulite and just rise above it and have fun together. Otherwise, what's the point of working so hard?

We were alone too long during COVID-19, and we got used to not making eye contact with others. In isolating ourselves for our safety, we lost our collective female community and the power that comes along with it. Find a way to open up again and make fierce friendships with like-minded women. We need one another.

The World Economic Forum published a white paper in May 2022 in which it states its recommendations for bringing employers and workers back to a "new normal" after the disruptions experienced over the last few years. My ultimate challenge to you would be, don't just fix what COVID-19 broke, but instead, build your organization up better than it ever was before the pandemic. We have a once in a lifetime opportunity to develop a new vision for the future of work in our country. Don't miss out!

You have already taken the first step by reading this book and helping me shine a light called empathy on the modern workforce. Now, you have a once in a lifetime opportunity to change your own organization. It's not complicated. It just takes learning a few new things and asking for help from someone who is qualified to help you devise a plan. You have come this far. Now I challenge you to take the next step.

The Good Work Framework: A new business agenda for the future of work aims to help companies establish a new benchmark for job quality by providing a consistent and goal-oriented approach to the development of comprehensive people strategies and to guide measurable actions to promote good work.[33]

The framework sets out five objectives and associated goals:

1. Promote fair pay and social justice
2. Provide flexibility and protection

---

33 *The Good Work Framework: A new business agenda for the future of work. (n.d.). Retrieved January 21, 2024, from World Economic Forum website: https://www.weforum.org/publications/the-good-work-framework-a-new-business-agenda-for-the-future-of-work/.*

3. Deliver on health and well-being
4. Drive diversity, equity, and inclusion
5. Foster employability and learning culture.

This is your new roadmap.

Try not to get lost along the way.

Use your GPS and listen to your Small, Quiet Voice.

They will both keep you on track.

THE END

DEDICATIONS

ANTHONY (TONY) (CONAN) LEE MEKEEL—This book is dedicated to my husband for standing by me and holding me up even after he was diagnosed with prostate cancer at just fifty years old. I was distraught and broken when I found out that the love of my life, a self-proclaimed workaholic, had a "preventable" cancer. Despite what people and doctors told me, I just knew his diagnosis stemmed from his high stress and demanding job coupled with his refusal to go to the doctor, the dentist, the optometrist, a therapist, a chiropractor, or even take an hour away from work each year for his annual checkup. "Self-care matters," I would persist. "If you can't love yourself, how can anyone else love you?" But the fact of the matter was that I did love him deeply, despite his apparent inability to love himself. It was complicated.

Self-care, scheduling time off for us, setting limitations at work; these were the things I had been begging him to do for himself since we first met ten years ago. Stress manifests in your body as disease and his answer for stress relief was more work, but when did it ever end? I saw him trapped in this hamster wheel and would pull him out when I could, but this man just loves to work. It's how he defines his worth. Providing for our family gave him his identity and he was good at it, but things had been off balance for way too long. When he was diagnosed with cancer at such a young age, I was not altogether surprised. Even though I had feared sickness or disease may rear its ugly head eventually, I was shocked at the timing of the diagnosis.

The word cancer used in the context of my person was something I had never even considered, much less have the need to worry about now. We were healthy. We took care of ourselves, and we had a long time together before we had to worry about getting sick and caring for one another like old people do.

The timing of this whole thing was terrible and like a slap in the face from God. Hadn't we both worked hard, given when we could and raised our sons in a way that honored God? After struggling, parenting, stressing, and budgeting for ten years without any help from the boys' dad, and no help from family because we live in Florida, he and I were about to finally be empty nesters.

Raising the boys was wonderful and it is time we both feel blessed to have spent guiding and loving them. Being their co-parents drew Tony and I closer together than most couples have to be. He was, and is, the center of my universe. Life has been a blur, but we thought now that we could just enjoy one another. Tony never even wanted kids, but he showed up for my three boys, day in and day out. He was the only consistent masculine role model they had for ten years.

I have a tremendous amount of respect and gratitude that he did that for me and my boys, and more than anything my heart's wish was for he and I to have more time to just enjoy one another. No kids, fewer distractions... we would finally get our honeymoon. But cancer... now? This cannot be. I was so terribly saddened and angry about his diagnosis. I felt cheated by God. "What do you mean, Tony has cancer? Check his test results again."

His diagnosis shook me to the core. We had only been together for ten years, married for two. As I let the news settle into my bones over the next few weeks, our new reality felt darker, sad, unsure, and frightening. For the first time since I had been with

Tony, I no longer felt safe. The word "cancer" would hurt my heart and take the air out of my lungs if I didn't stay busy. I know now that is one of the reasons that I had my nervous breakdown. I was trying to just stay as busy as possible, so I didn't have to deal with our reality. Being his wife was too scary and discouraging because I didn't yet have the tools to deal with being the prostate wife. But now I do, thank God.

IMPORTANT: MEN SHOULD ASK THEIR DOCTOR TO SCREEN FOR PROSTATE CANCER AT AGE 40. Doing so can save a life, like it did for my husband. Please spread the word about the risks and early symptoms of prostate cancer and encourage a PSA blood test that can easily be added to the annual blood test men should be getting every year. I know that you love the men in your life, so please share our story with them. Early detection of any disease saves lives. Men, if you don't want to go to the doctor for yourself, then please go for the people in your life who love you. We want you around for many, many years to come!

I share tools for the intimate partners of men with prostate cancer on my blog hosted on YouHaveArrivedBook.com. I have reluctantly become "The Prostate Wife," and it's a title I never wanted but one I proudly embrace as a responsibility now.[34] If you or someone you know is the intimate partner of a man being treated for prostate cancer, please tell them about this resource. I thought I was going crazy, and truth be told, I asked Tony for a divorce three times over the past year. I was miserable, but it does not have to be so hard.

What we have found, by having to clean up this mess that cancer so inconveniently created, was that we have grown closer as a

34 *Mekeel, S. (n.d.). The Prostate Wife - Dealing with Androgen Deprivation Therapy. Retrieved February 3, 2024, from prostatewife.blogspot.com website: https://prostatewife.blogspot.com/.*

couple in so many ways. We have seen where we were lacking in our relationship and had the chance to build it back better over the past year. Tony and I have risen to the occasion for the damn "C-Word," and if we can do THAT together as a couple, there is nothing we can't conquer together. A diagnosis should never mean a divorce, especially when you have a mermaid like me.

—Shannon Joy Mekeel

"MOTHER JONES"—I have only recently discovered this woman, but her story impacted me deeply. While intently listening to the universe, I stumbled across the biography of Mary G. Harris Jones (1837-1930).[35] Most people knew her as Mother Jones after she became a champion for workers' rights during the Industrial Revolution. She was born in Cork Ireland and immigrated to Canada with her family at the age of ten.

Fleeing the potato famine, the family settled in Toronto in 1847. Despite personal hardship and extreme poverty, Mother Jones would eventually become a champion for all Americans. She was an unlikely hero for others, mostly because she had experienced so much personal loss, and she didn't appear to be qualified for the roles that she played. In 1867, yellow fever took the lives of all four of her children and her husband. Mother Jones was a widow and alone by the age of thirty.

She persisted and started her life over again in Chicago where she built a successful dressmaking business, only to lose it all again in the Great Chicago Fire of 1871. Jones' next twenty years

35 *Mother Jones. (2020, February 14). Retrieved February 3, 2024, from Wikipedia website: https://en.wikipedia.org/wiki/Mother_Jones.*

were spent in obscurity. Not much was written about her during this time, but she was building a life, making friends, setting up a network of like-minded people, and helping where her heart would lead her. But mostly... Mother Jones listened. She heard a common grievance from everyone around her about the lack of safety policies and safe equipment at work. She listened to her friends talk about the cut-throat ways their bosses would terminate sick or injured employees and replace them with new workers who were oblivious to their corruption. Everyone around her had fallen victim to the Industrial Revolution.

This plight defined the time, and resistance to the machine was the cultural norm. Many thought the machine to be too powerful, and they were too tired and demoralized to do anything about it, but Mother Jones cared about the people, and she knew things had to change. Society simply could not proceed in its current state. So, Mother Jones made some noise. She worked tirelessly in the labor movement to protest the gruesome injustices described in Upton Sinclair's, *The Jungle*. Her life was defined by hard work, dealing with despair, listening, and then service to her fellow man.

Mother Jones became who she needed to be in each stage of her life and accomplished more than anyone would have ever guessed a female Irish immigrant could. Mother Jones was an unlikely hero. By the turn of the century, Jones had found the strength to brush herself off and fight. She pulled her hair back in a tight bun, and she got to work instituting change for the masses. By the turn of the century—twenty years before women were granted the right to vote—Mother Jones had become a respected and charismatic speaker of labor injustices.

She even became the cofounder of the Industrial Workers of the World (IWW). This book is dedicated to Mother Jones and all the other American agitators, male and female, since the seventeen hundreds. These brave souls sacrificed their livelihood, health, and in many cases, their lives to create necessary societal shifts. They all deserve better than to be forgotten in dusty, old history books. Let us learn from their strife and in so doing, NOT unravel their lives' work.

"Whatever the fight, don't be ladylike."

—Mother Jones

Finally, TO ALL THE MERMAIDS, thank you for your guidance and unconditional love Especially, as well, this memoir is dedicated to my sisters. Thank you for always believing in my goodness, my best intentions, and my talent as a writer and as a professional. Mom and Dad, I love you. To my brother, My Spark... you are a spiritual gift to me, and you always will be. Finally, to my stepparents, thank you for volunteering to raise my sister and me. You didn't have to sign up to parent someone else's kids, but I am so glad that you both did.

EVENTS THAT CAN BRING ABOUT A MIDLIFE CRISIS IN A WOMAN[36]

- Increased "crossover stressors" from multiple life roles
- Hormonal changes related to perimenopause or menopause
- Identity changes (i.e., identity crisis)
- Loss of fertility
- Family changes like empty nest syndrome
- Death of loved ones/friends
- Caregiving for partner
- Career disconnect or apathy
- Concerns about leaving behind a "legacy"

36 *Rockwell, L. (2022, December 23). Midlife Crisis in Women: Signs, Causes, & How to Cope. Retrieved February 3, 2024, from Choosing Therapy website: https://www.choosingtherapy.com/midlife-crisis-women/.*

ABOUT THE AUTHOR

SHANNON JOY MEKEEL is a proud USAF Veteran and in 2023 when this book was written, she was a marketing professional living in Florida who got fed up with inefficient processes, exasperated coworkers, and angry customers while also dealing with her husband's prostate cancer diagnosis and her youngest son's precarious graduation from high school. Shannon is now an organizational leadership thought leader, and the owner of SJM Consulting Services, where she shares her passion with organizations that need a healthy dose of empathy and want to fundamentally improve their culture and bottom line. Learn more at ShannonJoyMekeel.com.

www.ingramcontent.com/pod-product-compliance
Lightning Source LLC
Chambersburg PA
CBHW071319120626
46546CB00002B/380

9781959608691